Healing Our Worldview

HEALING

Our

WORLDVIEW

The Unity of Science and Spirituality

John Hitchcock

CHRYSALIS BOOKS

West Chester, Pennsylvania

Library of Congress Cataloging-in-Publication Data

Hitchcock, John L., 1936–
    Healing our worldview : unity of science and
    spirituality / John L. Hitchcock
        p.   cm.
    Includes bibliographical references and index.
    ISBN 0–87785–382–7
      1. Religion and science. 2. Spirituality. I. Title.
    BL240.2.H529   1999
    215—dc21   98–53135
                                                       CIP

Credits: Excerpts from *Joseph's Son* by Sheila Moon originally published by
Golden Quill Press are reprinted by permission from the Guild for
Psychological Studies Publishing House, San Francisco, California.

Edited by Stuart Shotwell
Designed by Michael Gunsleman Incorporated, Wilmington, Delaware
Set in Bodoni, Garamond italic, and Gill Sans Regular by Sans Serif, Inc.,
Saline, Michigan
Printed in the United States of America

Chrysalis Books is an imprint of the Swedenborg Foundation, Inc.
For more information, contact:
Chrysalis Books
Swedenborg Foundation Publishers
320 North Church Street
West Chester, PA 19380
(610) 430-3222 or http://www.swedenborg.com.

Contents

vii   Preface

xiii   Introduction

3   The Worldfield

26   The Transformation of Science

47   The Rise of Complementarity

69   The Divergence of Science and Religion

85   The Mythic Roots of Consciousness

106   The Cultural Path toward Convergence

128   Taking the Universe Inside

146   Religion: Binding Back Together

161   Unity

183   Appendix: The Anthropic Principle and the
        Web of the Universe

195   Notes

200   References

205   Index

Preface

The publication of this book by the Swedenborg Foundation gives me an opportunity to pay a debt of long standing to Emanuel Swedenborg himself. I have made a second career of furthering the convergence of science and spirituality, using ideas and constructs that were available to me primarily because of my Swedenborgian background. The Foundation is the appropriate partner for the repayment of this debt, because my work, like that of the Foundation, does not parallel or promote the work of any ecclesiastical organization. I like to think of my workshops and books as part of a noninstitutional movement that manifests the growth of human spirituality; and I have become convinced that Swedenborg saw his own work in the same light.

Swedenborg's place in the development of modern thought is pivotal, even though he has been relatively unknown. For two centuries, artists and writers have employed his ideas, even when it was very much out of fashion to mention his name. Over the years, I have heard numerous anecdotes about careers derailed when someone acknowledged Swedenborg's influence. I feel all the more obligation, therefore, to acknowledge my debt to him here.

As life becomes more complex, we must find ways to see through the mass of detail to the essentials, to the wholeness of things, and yet still take those details themselves into account—we must recognize "the ten thousand things," as the Chinese put it. The conflicting demands of living in the world as it is require that we continually find new ways to remind ourselves of that totally encompassing wholeness that some term "God" and many great scientists have called "the central order of things."[1] In my own work, I call it the "worldfield" or "the patterning," depending on whether the focus is on its substance or its form. Swedenborg referred to this duality as "divine love" and "divine wisdom," which I also like, though I prefer to use more neutral terms for general audiences.

A large part of our present worldview is influenced by the scientific rationalism of the past several centuries. In my opinion, this worldview is precisely what now stands in the way of seeing the wholeness of reality. At present it seems that we are for the most part unable to see the limitations of this rationalism and the ways in which it diminishes our humanity. Its effects are reflected in our obsession with statistics as measures of what we think we "really" know. In the twentieth century, experimental physics has uncovered phenomena that demonstrate clearly (clearly, that is, if we are open to seeing it) the fact that physical reality is nonrational at root.

If we are to incorporate this new knowledge into the way we live, however, merely seeking scientific justification for a new way of seeing reality, important as that is, will not suffice. We will also need a cultural evolution—a change in the emotional underpinnings of our intellectual life. In previous books I have focused on the scientific justification of and motivation for the emerging transformation of our way of seeing the world. In this book I will limit coverage of that topic to a brief summary. Here the focus instead will be on the cultural evolution that is necessary if we are to develop a new paradigm.

When both science and the worldview of our culture come to better alignment with the available facts, then individuals can incorporate new ways of seeing into their lives. However, this will require considerable effort if a real change in how we live is to occur. That is where the work of the pioneering psychologist C. G. Jung comes in. Jung saw that, for any understanding of the unity of reality to be assimilated into our lives, our understanding of ourselves must be consistent with our understanding of the universe. To that end, he worked with Wolfgang Pauli, one of the greatest physicists of the twentieth century, to find those consistencies. As I see it, Jung's is the only psychology so far to act upon such concerns, and the only view of human nature that is, in fact, consistent with the view of the universe that has arisen in modern physics. That is, Jung's view is at one with the worldview to which we seem to be coming and which this book aims to help bring to greater consciousness.

Changes in worldview, such as we are now undergoing, require two essential conditions: (1) a set of new facts, or newly recognized facts, that indicate the need for the change; and (2) a cultural environment in which these facts can be seen and accepted. There will always be individuals who see things that others do not, but until there is a readiness for a general understanding, those individuals, however prescient, will remain alien in the perception of the majority. What is now needed is not so much a statement of scientific facts, however clear, but rather an appeal to values, for we are not primarily intellectual beings. As Swedenborg put it, we are what we love, that is our very life. And Richard Cytowic, in his book *The Man Who*

Tasted Shapes, has given us a strong scientific case for the primacy of our emotional being, as anticipated by Swedenborg.[2]

Our growth toward the conscious participation of our emotional nature is not so much a problem as a promise. Our feelings are the repository of our wholeness; we cannot live on a merely intellectual basis. The problem, then, is that of *feeling* the reality and responding to it emotionally, in spite of all that we have assumed to be true. To be sure, we must assimilate intellectually the facts with which science provides us, but we must also become emotionally aware—that is, open our hearts to the new worldview presented here.

In 1946, Einstein said that we need to find a new manner of thinking if humanity is to survive.[3] Since that time, many have brought forth candidates for this new manner of thinking, from various religious perspectives to "new age thinking." This book is another offering, having the symbolic advantage of coming from a corner in which Einstein himself would not have looked: paradox. At the same time, Einstein is generally credited with uncovering the very paradoxical nature of physical reality that he implicitly repudiated in his often-quoted assertion that God does not play dice with the universe. That is, Einstein believed in a universe of clear concepts and unambiguous causality, as well as in the purely objective nature of physical reality. It is now widely agreed that he was mistaken on all of these counts. However, I do not believe that he was wrong about the need for new ways of thinking.

Disciplined paradoxical thinking has definite structure. It is not at all a failure of effort, but requires rather an intensification of effort. Established physical facts are now forcing us toward a paradoxical interpretation of reality. The layperson can hardly comprehend the sweat and anguish that has gone into the attempts of scientists to salvage a rationalistic view of physical reality. The emerging view is one of the most worked over, and most reluctantly accepted, eventualities in human intellectual history.

One of the most important aspects of paradoxical thinking is that it calls for a willingness to think in negative terms. For example, the experiments that have led us to apply the logically contradictory concepts of "wave" and "particle" to microphysical entities such as the electron are negative in structure: one experiment proves that the electron cannot be a wave, while another proves that the electron cannot be a particle. At the same time, we must have some concepts with which to describe what is going on in a positive manner, hence "wave" and "particle." At least we can say that things behave *like* waves or *like* particles, but then we must also acknowledge that we are making something of a makeshift, even a mythic, statement about reality. Such positive concepts govern everything that we do, including the making of devices with which to conduct the above experiments. What this means, however, is that all concepts by means of which we describe our world and our living are provisional to some degree.

Jung makes the point over and over that our concepts are partial, and that our attempt to grasp one aspect of a thing conceptually, important as that is, generally makes us focus instead on other aspects of the same thing. Because this point is so important, I will quote a few examples, including Jung's recognition of the parallel in physics:

I strive quite consciously for ambiguity of expression, because it is superior to unequivocalness and reflects the nature of life. My whole temperament inclines me to be very unequivocal indeed. That is not difficult, but it would be at the cost of truth.

Oddly enough the paradox is one of our most valuable spiritual possessions, while uniformity of meaning is a sign of weakness.

. . . Non-ambiguity and non-contradiction are one-sided and thus unsuited to express the incomprehensible.

Even the physicist is compelled by experience to make antinomian statements when he wants to give a concrete description of transcendental facts, such as the nature of light or of the smallest particles of matter, which he represents both as corpuscles and as waves.[4]

We will see Kierkegaard's similar assessment of paradox in chapter 6. Paradox actually liberates us from the prison of intellectualism and returns us to our humanity. We can no longer hide behind some external authority, but must take responsibility for our statements.

Acknowledgments

First thanks are due to David Eller, former executive director of the Swedenborg Foundation, for the invitation and the idea for me to do this book. Susan Poole, who worked with me initially on redoing the first draft, gave much toward ensuring clarity, and I am deeply in her debt. I know that I am not the world's easiest person to work with. Other readers with known contributions to the process include Carol Lawson and Ros Pickhardt. It is a great pleasure for me to reflect, as the project nears its end, on the immense value of their presence in my life and work. Stuart Shotwell not only did a beautiful job of editing and integrating the style, but has greatly boosted my morale in critical moments. Without the deep support of Alice B. Skinner, president of the Foundation, I would never have been in a position to do this work. Most of all, my wife, Carrie, has held me in spirit through the difficulties that I impose upon myself in writing a book.

Introduction

This book is about science and spirituality, or science and religion—or whatever expression is most comfortable to you. I will not be speaking for any established point of view within either of these areas of human concern. Science and religion (or spirituality) are very different ways of knowing and/or relating to reality. I want to show that, although they have been seen as pointing to different realities, they actually complement each other, for behind or beyond each perception of reality lies a world in which all realities are unified.

This unitary world cannot be perceived by us as it is in itself. It discloses itself through the kinds of contrasts that are accessible to our conscious minds, that is, in terms of polarities or opposites. In order to approach even a beginning appreciation of this world, we must transcend our normal rationality as well as we can, by trying to hold these opposites together in our minds. With practice, we can make progress in doing so.

The proponents of each of the two ways of perceiving and relating to reality have tended to stress the differences between them, and to favor one rather than the other, even to the point of seeing them as being at war with each other. Healing our worldview, then, requires recognizing the ultimate unity of two apparently disparate realities. I believe that we are ready to open ourselves to see that unity, and to begin to incorporate that openness into our living.

More than any of my previous writings on the subject, this book sketches historically the developments of science and spirituality as they apply to the unity and disunion of the two. We will look back as much as five thousand years in history. And we will follow different historical threads in different chapters, sometimes a factual thread, sometimes a conceptual one, sometimes a mythic. Our method will be akin to the use of flashbacks in telling a story. The developments that will enter into the flow are those that are most important to the overall movement of science and spirituality.

Before we begin, however, I offer an overview of the course we are to take. I encourage the reader to peruse this brief summary first in order to get his or her first bearings on the journey toward a new worldview. To simplify the presentation, I have reserved most of the documentation of sources for the full treatment in the main chapters of the book.

Chapter 1: The Worldfield

Worldfield is a name for the unitary reality that forms a "background" to the visible world and produces all that exists. The worldfield is a spirit-matter totality that is alive, that is the source of all life, and that we sometimes refer to as God. To our contrast-based ego-consciousness, it is the transcendent realm, but it is also immanent, which is to say that it is our innermost depths. The word *field* is used to suggest that the unitary background to perceived reality is vast and that it constitutes the interconnections of all things. It encompasses all, both from without and within.

This chapter will draw most upon the work of psychologist Erich Neumann, a colleague of C. G. Jung, who has done the most to develop conceptually the idea of the unitary reality that Jung called the *unus mundus* (Latin for "one world," or "world of unity"). Both of these terms are attempts to be more circumspect in referring to God the creator, more inclusive of worldviews outside the various religions.

The chapter presents a simple model for the origination of all things from within the worldfield by means of the emergence of opposites. The unity of opposites is a *nonrational* unity. We see things, literally or figuratively, by contrast, in which opposites, such as dark and light, are separate. Therefore we see both of the opposites, such as the light part and the dark part. The appearance of opposites is the product of our human ego-consciousness. Yet, as we will see, that same ego-consciousness is the source of our freedom. It is a sort of distancing from the immediacy of nonrational reality, so that we can function rationally, with choice.

The rationalistic universe of standard science has not been large and open enough to encompass all that comprises our world. Thus it threatens the very unity of the universe in our minds. Specifically, it has excluded spirit and meaning, and even consciousness itself. In fact, the present foundations of physics exclude even life. However, certain events link our inner and outer worlds precisely by creating meaning in their coincidence. Jung used the term *synchronicity* for this kind of event.

In an attempt to begin to break down the rigidity of our present worldview, the opposites "inner" and "outer" are shown equally to be products of our ego-consciousness, along with other opposites; they are not necessarily attributes of the "world" itself. By means of our seeing things in terms of opposites we gain freedom and adaptability, but we still do not know things as they are in the worldfield.

Chapter 2: The Transformation of Science

Scientists are generally divided into two camps: experimentalists and theoreticians, for whom I develop the metaphor of mechanics and mystics, respectively. Following Carl Sagan, I am using the term *mystic* here in a negative sense, namely, the uncritical imaginative stance which says that we can know the world without observing it. This has nothing to do with religious mysticism as the direct perception of things beyond our earthly sight and comprehension. The division between experimentalists and theoreticians has been with us from the very beginning of western science in the sixth century B.C.E. in Ionia, which lies across the Aegean Sea from Greece.

The first half of this chapter presents three major transformations of science in terms of the mechanics and mystics involved: Thales and Pythagoras in ancient Greece, Kepler and Galileo in the seventeenth century, and Bohr and Einstein in our own times. In each case, the major transformation was brought about through honoring observation over theory. Thales introduced science itself as the discovery of patterns in nature; Kepler, honoring the observations of Tycho Brahe, overcame the notion that the orbits of the planets must be composed of circles; and Bohr's complementarity displaced the deterministic world of Einstein.

Our current scientific worldview does not merely influence our cultural outlook; it is a powerful determinant as to how we see things in the first place. At present, a major shift of scientific paradigm is underway, though the change is being strongly resisted, and not least by the scientific community itself. This change is the transition from rationalistic to holistic thinking.

The second half of this chapter expands on the third transformation of science described in the first half. It sets forth the power and limitations of rationalism/reductionism, and describes the model of complementarity that is in process of superseding it. It also points out the fact that scientific concepts are never more than an approximation of the "truth." The evolution of worldview is an endless process in principle, because we discover new phenomena through experimentation and observation that could never be anticipated by thought alone.

Chapter 3: The Rise of Complementarity

The idea of the world as a complex of opposites goes back, in the East, to Chinese yin-yang symbolism developed in the second millennium B.C.E., and, in the West, to Anaximander of the Ionian school. Between them lies India, absolutely permeated with the clash between dualism and nondualism.

After defining complementarity, this chapter describes the ancient roots of that concept: first, in the Chinese *Book of Changes;* and second, in the Grecian philosopher Anaximander's concept of the indefinite, from which all warring opposites arise and to which they return. In the Greek view, this source of opposites is related to the divine, as it certainly was in China as well.

In each pair of opposites, one member tends to divide and separate things, while the other is of an inclusive nature. For instance, our intellectual side is separative, while our emotional side is inclusive. A theological example is given from a sermon by Paul Tillich, in which sin is seen as the separative member and grace as the inclusive member of the pair.

Paradigm shifts, changes in our apprehension of the

world, are not matters of intellectual understanding alone, but must include our feeling assent. The latter is shown by our changing the way we live. Since the shift currently underway is moving from rationalism to complementarity, it is natural that the rational side resists the change.

By itself the rational side of our brain cannot perceive or respond to the wholeness of things, which is the province of the other side of the human brain. In fact, we possess many nonrational ways of knowing, and these are now wanting to be heard. The way of *healing* the disjunction between the rational and the nonrational, just as in the case of other psychological issues, is to try to get the isolated part to see the need for wholeness, and to do that requires that we speak to it as much as possible on its own terms.

Therefore, part of this chapter is devoted to considering the phenomena in physics that brought complementarity into the question: how wholeness intervened in our picture of the electrons as they act in atoms. In atoms, electrons are in their wave state—that is, they act as if they are continuous waves, not discrete particles. Although the wave state is real, physicists often prefer to view electrons as particles that somehow travel in a general pattern given by the wave description of matter.

In the case of this wave/particle paradox, physical facts necessitated the letting go of rationalism in science, but the paradigm of the rationalistic world is so deeply ingrained in our psyches that we have not been able to stop applying rationalistic one-sidedness to the way that we live. Therefore, the chapter closes with a strong statement to the effect that the physical universe is not obliged to uphold our rationalistic assumptions and that logic is not the basis of being. The harshness of rationalism must be softened for us to grow further in humanity.

Chapter 4: The Divergence of Science and Religion

The coming convergence of science and spirituality (or religion), must be seen as a reconnection of the two, since they arose together in the human psyche. This chapter is a survey that deals with the original unity of science and religion and explains how that unity gradually came apart over several millennia. The realization that certain events (such as solar eclipses) occur as patterns in nature, and thus do not necessarily indicate divine displeasure, was perhaps the first major break. In this chapter we also look especially at the Middle Ages and the Enlightenment.

The use of reason to eliminate the unreasonable in the investigation of nature proved so powerful that, for many, it displaced the divine, as that was then understood, in its very numinosity, its power to generate awe. Another truly awe-inspiring aspect of the rationalistic search for the nature of things is the measurability of physical reality. With our many means of measurement, we humans have gained immense freedom and power, and many have felt this as a liberation from intellectual enslavement to religious dogma. Feelings such as these are probably behind the deification of the rational in the one-sided extreme of rationalism. The rebalancing of our worldview by seeing wholes along with seeing parts is nonrational, a way of holding opposites in view simultaneously.

In the push to rationalism, the divine has been eclipsed, but in the healing it becomes visible once again. Reason has been seen as a threat to faith, but that cannot ultimately be the case. Science and religion must be seen as two aspects of the same human enterprise, since they both seek to discover the basis of our being and the reasons that things are as they are. Because we now know, on the basis of scientifically established fact, that the universe is nonrational, and therefore that rationalism can never master it, reason can once again be seen as a divine gift, not at all antithetical to the gifts of the spirit, including inspired writings.

Chapter 5: The Mythic Roots of Consciousness

This chapter takes up the theme of chapter 1 and carries it further, now that we have followed three threads of the evolution of consciousness in chapters 2, 3, and 4. The mythic images given here in chapter 5, from Greek, Egyptian, Maori, and Chinese cultures, show us deeper, parallel layers of the model of how opposites emerge from the worldfield.

The differentiation of opposites, through which science and religion came to be seen first as different, and then as in opposition to each other, is part of a general process in the evolution of consciousness. Its mythological roots take the form of the motif of the *separation of the world-parents*, earth and sky (heaven). This separation is also equivalent to the expulsion from Eden in Judeo-Christian texts.

The differentiation of science and religion, representing matter and spirit, respectively, follows the same model. Separation precedes a reunion that has increased meaning, as a wound precedes healing. In the mythic material, the separation of the world-parents makes *eros,* attractive love, visible. After the separation, love goes to work to reunite that which has been parted.

To put it differently, love initiates a process of gathering those aspects of reality to which we are attracted. Love is the mover of all human curiosity and meaningful world building, but *we* are the final products, as individually formed beings. This gathering together is the process of correcting our projections, our automatic untested assumptions as to the way things really are. When we merely assume that things are as we think they are, we fail to actually take them in; we say that we are *projecting* our own reality onto the environment. Really taking things in requires our openness to reassessment of ourselves, others, and the world.

The second half of the chapter opens a description of the process of gathering consciousness and the role of symbols in the process. This theme will be picked up and developed more fully in chapter 7, after the last (cultural) thread, the last "flashback," is followed out in chapter 6. The material of the two chapters (5 and 7) is based largely on Marie-Louise von Franz's book, *Projection and Recollection in Jungian Psychology: Reflections of the Soul*.[1]

We are engaged in a process of deepening human consciousness to the point where we can truly integrate our feelings and our knowledge, our hearts and our minds, our spirituality and our science. Our minds can easily assimilate knowledge in the rational mode, but what really counts is not what we know, but how we live. That generally requires a moral, integrative act, a painful acceptance of where and how we have been mistaken.

Chapter 6: The Cultural Path toward Convergence

This chapter deals with the cultural roots of the understanding of complementarity in the modern era, beginning with Swedenborg's description of God as divine love and wisdom. An independent root can be seen in a saying of Kierkegaard's, "existence is contradiction." Kierkegaard provided physicist Niels Bohr with the mental model for complementarity, which in turn gave Pierre Teilhard de Chardin the notion of "spirit-matter." The new vision of wholeness, via the ultimate unity of opposites, culminates in the work of C. G. Jung, who with help from physicist Wolfgang Pauli drew the scientific and the spiritual together in such a way that we could use their unity to live differently. A sketch of this living worldview is given.

The cultural evolution of the past three centuries has actually enabled scientists to bring forth and interpret new experimental facts. In previous chapters I make the point that even now the cultural bias toward rationalism is blocking the path to the inevitable interpretation of complementarity as the nonrational unity of opposites. Perhaps our current worldview is softening enough that something nonrational is not such an emotional threat. Scientists are as liable to bias as any of the rest of us. They, like the rest of us, come to see things differently only when they are forced to do so by facts. In part, that is as it should be, but whether scientists or not we also can learn to question our views to determine where we might be deluding ourselves and to be bolder in seeking what might be a more comprehensive view.

Cultural history is very complex, and only a few threads will be brought to view in this chapter. However, an understanding of the cultural component is extremely important.

Chapter 7: Taking the Universe Inside

Science has been the study of universals; its focus thus tends to neglect our individual uniqueness as humans. On the other hand, we need always a more comprehensive view of the cosmos, and thus we need our science as well. In two ways, we take the universe inside in the process of individuation: in opening ourselves to the universe as it is (correcting our projections concerning outer reality) and in building our inner being by turning inwards. Since, as we are learning, the inner/outer dichotomy is not ultimately the truth, we thus complete the circle with which we began.

We can learn who we are only by differentiating ourselves from what we see. As we begin our journey of self-discovery, we generally assume (unconsciously) that the world is
just what we think it is. Only by discovering that we are wrong,
that we are projecting ourselves onto the world, can we at last
admit to what we project, and thus also see the world more
truthfully.

This chapter includes a view of the development of
human consciousness from infancy and even before. In the beginning there is almost nothing "within." There is only the "archaic identity of subject and object," including the whole
universe. The infant is at one with the universe, God, the Self,
the worldfield. This state is known psychologically as "infantile omnipotence." But as the infant encounters "reality," it
learns gradually that it is one thing and the world another.

However, this learning process is lifelong. There are
always untested projections included in our worldview. We can
always learn more deeply who we are and what the world is.
One especially profound learning now available to us is to perceive the embeddedness of spirit, or the divine, in all things.

The development of the gastrointestinal tract in early
human embryology provides a model and metaphor for the
combination of turning inward and opening to the reality that
we must undergo to take new steps in evolution. I call this process "involution." From a hollow sphere of cells, the embryo
turns half inside-out to make a tube with which it can take in
food from the outside world; what was "skin" takes on a diges-
tive function. Psychologically speaking, we must turn inward
in order to receive spiritual nourishment from the inner/outer
totality.

On a spiritual level, the same process parallels the
gathering in of what we have projected, for our spiritual con-
solidation and nourishment. Ultimately, the metaphor also

applies to the psychological/spiritual death-rebirth process. As a culture, we have projected our aliveness onto a world beyond physical death, and so have missed the real meaning of human aliveness in this world. Jesus said that to come alive we must destroy the walls around our psyche that we have built up.[2] Dying to be reborn is something we must encounter many times in our physical lives, and in submitting to that process, the fundamental aliveness of the universe can flow through us.

Chapter 8: Religion: Binding Back Together

Whatever helps us to reestablish our creative relationship to the basis of our being makes up the content and meaning of the word *religion*. We saw in chapter 4 how the advance of rationalism caused a fading of our contact with the divine. The task now is to find once again our depth and our wholeness.

It is up to us to create the realm of God by giving God the sovereignty over our lives. We have anticipated such a coming apart from our doing much to bring it about. That such an attitude is nonviable is a major theme of the chapter.

The largest theme in binding back together, though, is the role of forgiveness, both *by* and *for* ourselves. Because our spiritual maturity is only attained at the cost of suffering, we must *forgive the universe* for the fact that this is the case. A universe that is intended to bring forth love seems only able to do so by setting for us problems that only love can solve. The fact that we tend to accept our status quo and not to push ourselves closer to our potential is one major reason that we need forgiveness. Our relationships also give us many opportunities to need to be forgiven, and that softens us to the reality of a loving God. True humanity is a condition of being vulnerable.

There is something at work in the totality of things that is leading us toward a goal of individuation and consciousness.

That consciousness includes awareness of the depths of reality and its numinosity. Psychologically, this process is known as "centroversion." Hidden within all things, God is waiting for us to come to ourselves, become open, and see the grace and beauty of what we have been given.

Chapter 9: Unity

This chapter is my attempt to say how I believe science, religion, and living itself might be different if the vision I have presented were to come to general acceptance.

The rationalistic attitude in science fostered human alienation; the fall of rationalism shows that in order to be truly aligned with reality, we must reenter creation with our whole being. Rootlessness and despair have deeply infected humanity, both individually and collectively. What religion suggests is that a direct human sense of *being required* now appears to be calling us, through science, toward a new aliveness.

The convergence of science and religion is not something that occurs in the mind alone, in the realm of pure ideas, but in human lives and hearts. Both are about how to live as a part of the universe, in alignment with reality, or they are nothing. At the same time, in the convergence of science and religion, the very concept of a universe, if that is what everything adds up to, demands the unity of God. The evidence is more and more insistent that the cosmos is unified and whole. Thus we must push our monotheism as far as it can go. Neither science nor religion alone can hope for success in this work; they cannot really do without each other. The wholeness or completeness of humanity, both in individuals and in the whole species, is at stake.

The assumption that humanity is a special creation (see chapter 1) still pervades philosophy, law, theology, and science. One way to combat our unconscious assumptions in this area is to think about the whole long evolution of life while also thinking about the divine at work in the process. The cosmos evolved for over four billion years before humans appeared. Was God impatient or lonely during that interval? The nonrational nature of reality ensures an *open-ended* evolutionary process, with new species superseding humanity endlessly and with increasing consciousness. There can be no final tableau.

The idea that God's consciousness is new and growing, that God is awakening, accords with the picture of evolution, and begins to make sense of many issues in theology that are problems only when one assumes that creation is rational.

The individual component in religious experience means that religious pluralism must be our course, while science speaks to the things that we know together and as a whole. In the end, however, the only thing that counts is how we live as humans. The diversity that the universe can encompass is just one way in which the universe sets problems for us that only love can solve.

Healing Our Worldview

CHAPTER ONE

The Worldfield

To see a World in a Grain of Sand
And a Heaven in a Wild Flower
Hold Infinity in the palm of your hand
And Eternity in an hour
—William Blake, "Auguries of Innocence"

Most of us have had a fleeting realization of the *oneness* of things from time to time, perhaps akin to the feeling that inspired William Blake. These are the mysterious moments when everything seems transparent and the interconnections of all things become visible.

We need a word for the web of connectedness that gives us those glimpses of a deeper reality. One image that readily evokes the mystery of spirit is a large meadow with grass rippling as the wind passes down it. The word *field* holds many associations, including the abundance of life that grows from the ground. We use the word also for areas of interest or study. And physicists also use the word for nonmaterial connections such as the force that a magnet exerts on a fleck of iron, or that with which the Earth draws all material things to fall toward it.

The field in question, however, is the most vast of all. It is that whose force emanated in the creation of the cosmos, and it also remains present in every created thing. Let us call it the *worldfield*.

What kinds of images are aroused by the term *worldfield*? Some sort of hidden knowledge? A force that might shape the becoming of things? A guide for our living? All the knowledge still to be disclosed? The power of a god or goddess? Scripture, such as John 1:1, "In the beginning was the Word"? In its own way, each of these images is appropriate to the direction in which we will be going; our quest will take us to the root of our freedom, creativity, and wholeness, and will illuminate the path toward the integration of all our parts.

In itself, the name *worldfield* does not explicitly express the ultimate *unity* of all that is and of the principle that gives rise to creation. Two other names have been used in the attempt to find a term that is both simple and comprehensive: *the unitary reality* and the Latin term *unus mundus*. I will use both of these terms from time to time. The latter might be translated "the world of unity," keeping the ideas of "one" *(unus)* and "world" *(mundus)*, the latter in the sense of the Greek *cosmos*, an ordering principle opposed to *chaos*, also a Greek notion.

Fields

Fields are present everywhere we look. In every sense of wonder or of the holy, we *feel* the field. Wherever we see the power and interconnectedness of life, we feel the field. In a tree-bordered farm, in hot-water plumes in ocean depths, or with lizards and insects in deserts, we see forms of life appropriate to each habitat, and so we perceive the working of the field. And we see it in the patterns of give and take, eating and being eaten, migration, and all the other patterns, so abundant in nature. Creatures are one with their settings, and that whole-ness is the unity of that part of the field.

But such instances are only the beginning. The field is present in all religious experience and in every spiritual aspi-ration. It has many components, many levels. Each of us, though we seem to be such separate beings, is bound to a field of origin, and through that field to the worldfield.

All life has arisen from a common source; that much is evident from the uniformity of the life-process, mediated and informed by DNA in every case. That this source is a patterned field is also indicated by the very uniformity of the laws of na-ture throughout the observable universe. The same elements are present in the most distant galaxies as are present here.

Of course, since it has become clear that the universe originated in a great explosion known as the Big Bang, we know that at the moment of its origin, the whole cosmos was virtually a point. This could help to explain why the cosmos is so uniform in its patterning. The field that gave birth to it has encompassed it everywhere from the beginning.

We speak of the patterning of the field for at least two reasons. The first is variety. On the earth alone, many millions of species exist within the unity that we call by the single word *life*. These different life forms arise because of the variety of environments on the earth, but also because each environment is an ecosystem. Simply to have a life cycle, a species must have something to feed on that is also a life form (plant or an-imal), and it is most successful when there is a great variety of forms for it to draw on. For example, giant pandas eat bamboo shoots almost exclusively. If they live among a variety of bam-boo that dies after producing fruit, and the entire bamboo forest synchronizes on a cycle in which it all dies after a cer-tain number of years, the pandas will be in great danger in the period before the next cycle of bamboo growth begins.

Every pattern of biological being is drawn from the field, and was therefore present (in a virtual sense) from the start. This is true not only of the life-forms that already exist, but of all those others that are merely possible on earth or that are possible in any other planetary environment in the universe.

The second reason we speak of the patterning of the field is that the creation of the physical cosmos came about by means of opposites, which came into being in the Big Bang. All the properties of matter come in opposing pairs, such as positive and negative electric charge. We also experience the act of living in terms of opposites, such as inner/outer, risk/security, self/other, heart/mind, and spirit/matter, among others. Why are these pairs just what they are? Because when placed together in a unified world, they suggest a patterning of the whole.

The worldfield is ultimately called into conception to explain the mystery of how things are connected, in spite of their separation into distinct entities and concepts. An example of this connectedness is the unity of animals with their habitats in spite of their separateness as individuals. The idea of the worldfield can explain not only the unity of the physical laws of the universe, but also parapsychological phenomena and the meaningful relatedness of seemingly random events, such as meeting just the right person at just the right time.

More than this, the field concept holds the key to how consciousness grew in a cosmos that began as unconscious "matter." By consciousness I mean the consciousness of humans and other creatures, not a potential consciousness of God or of the worldfield itself. In humans, we have two forms: ego-consciousness, which is our everyday self-reflexive awareness of things in terms of contrasts, and a deeper consciousness, through which the ego is linked to the field.

Science itself needs and uses the concept of fields, applying it to phenomena ranging from the infinite reach of gravity through the phenomena of electricity and magnetism, to the very nonrational nature of microphysical entities such as electrons and photons. Microphysical fields give characteristic shapes to atoms and molecules; biological fields guide the formation of embryos and the life cycles of species, including, for example, the transformation of caterpillars into butterflies. On a larger scale are the migration patterns of animals, birds, and butterflies again, which crisscross significant portions of the planet. The parents of salmon are dead when the young are born, but the offspring will travel widely and return to the same stream, the same pool, to spawn and die, clearly operating within some type of field. Rupert Sheldrake's work with homing pigeons similarly suggests that these birds are simply "connected" to their loft and can find it even if it is moved. The notion of "morphogenetic fields" (as described by physicist Michael Polanyi in his book *Personal Knowledge*, and experimentally developed later by Sheldrake) is very relevant to our examination of the worldfield.[1] The interest in these larger fields seems to point to a *zeitgeist* that is still in the process of self-revelation, since many researchers began working independently on these fields in the 1950s.

In one sense, all fields are *environmental* fields, for they are, by definition, encompassing.

A Model of How Things Emerge from the Field

For over seven decades it has been growing ever more clear that electrons and photons can behave in such ways that to describe them with any completeness requires us to assign them certain properties that are mutually contradictory. Our knowledge of the oppositeness embodied in the nature of subatomic particles (of which we take photons and electrons only as the simplest examples) is among the most secure scientific knowledge that we possess. We say that an electron or a photon can behave sometimes as if it were a wave and sometimes as if it were a particle. This is called wave-particle duality.

Very simply, a wave is something connected with its surroundings, while a particle is something disconnected. Logically, a thing cannot be both connected and disconnected. Thus these properties are opposites, but though opposites they are properties of *one thing*. This contradiction compels us to develop some means of accounting for the unity of the opposites.

If opposites are bound together, as they are in physics (and psychology and other fields as well), there must be something that encompasses them and even gives them birth. This has been strongly intuited by ancients of both Western and Eastern traditions. In Greece, in the sixth century B.C.E., Anaximander postulated what he called the *apeiron*, or the "boundless," as the source of things that have opposing natures, a concept very like the worldfield. In the eleventh century B.C.E., the Duke of Chou in China, classically regarded as the compiler of the *I Ching*, or *Book of Changes*, gave great impetus to the philosophy of yin and yang, the general opposites whose nature pervades all things and events. These opposites are bound together in an eternal dance of cycles, represented by the symbol shown in Figure 1.1. Taken together, the opposites form a whole. This symbol will be discussed more in chapter 3.

The simplest sort of thing that we can envision as a model would be something like Figure 1.2. We will use the example of the electron and generalize it to the model itself.

In the field, as I have been saying, the electron is itself in its wholeness. This is the upper part of the diagram. In the visible realm of science (and our ego-consciousness), the field shows us two aspects, wave and particle. The aspects of

Figure 1.1: T'ai Chi T'u, the Diagram of the Great Ultimate

life that we experience as opposites, some of which were mentioned above, follow the same pattern. In the generalized model on the right, visible aspect A contrasts with visible aspect B. Both aspects connect with the field, or overlap the field, but they are separate from each other. Aspect A (of life) could be our intellectual side and Aspect B our emotional side, both of which are part of our wholeness in general. In the Chinese example, above, Aspect A could be "yang" and Aspect B could be "yin."

One of the most important example pairs we will be dealing with is spirit-matter. If we combine the spirit and matter aspects of reality, what we get in the field realm is the field itself.

In the sense of the model, the electron as it is in itself, in its wholeness, is a field-entity. Our choice of physical experiments determines which aspect it will show us. *In physics as in life, our choices determine what we will see.*

The field connects opposites, from the complementary quantities that are bound together in physics to the great opposites of human living mentioned earlier. These opposites have arisen in that form or aspect of consciousness that we know as ego-consciousness, which is also the principal tool of science.

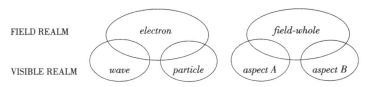

FIELD REALM — *electron* — *field-whole*

VISIBLE REALM — *wave* / *particle* — *aspect A* / *aspect B*

Figure 1.2

More important, however, is the fact that struggling with these opposites constitutes the problems of living. The fact that we must struggle so keeps us conscious of values. In the absence of problems, we are no longer challenged and we "go unconscious."

It should perhaps be emphasized at this point that the opposites are our *characteristically human* perceptions. We have no reason to conclude in advance that other conscious species divide up the world in the same way. Contrasts make it possible for us to perceive and deal with reality. The insight that we construct a world in our own particular way applies to any of the pairs of opposites, and we will use the opposites "inner" and "outer" below in an extensive and important example. The insight applies to "good" and "evil" as well, though in the case of these opposites we have much experience to the effect that even different human societies view this pair very diversely; acts that are good in one society are evil in another. If we think about how diversely humans view constructs even of the same general dimension of living (in this case, the moral dimension of good and evil), we will be better able to see the truth of the insight that any of the pairs of opposites can be defined in different ways.

How might we apply our model to the good/evil pair? (See Figure 1.3.) Shall we call the field here a "general moral dimension"?

The particular contrasts that we construct help us to see the world around and within us, but at the same time, they limit our seeing.

Fields and Freedom

Ego-consciousness functions by two complementary means. On the one hand, we become aware of contrasts, and on the

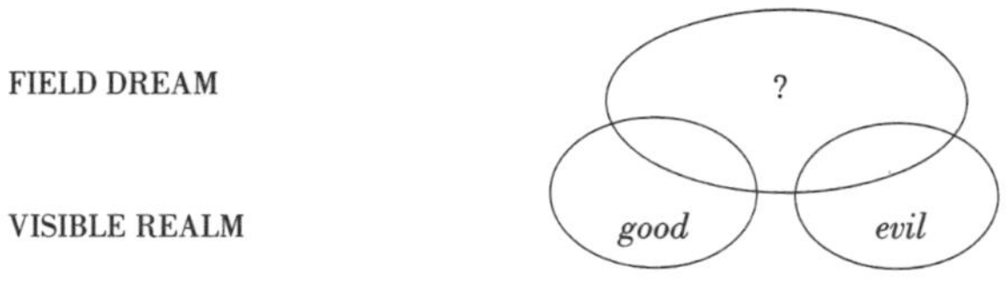

FIELD DREAM

VISIBLE REALM

Figure 1.3

other, we grasp wholes. But even seeing a whole within a larger field of view employs a contrast similar to that of figure and background in a work of art. Thus, generally speaking, our ego-consciousness is a consciousness of contrasts, and I often refer to it as contrast-consciousness, to distinguish it from our possible awareness of things in the field to which contrast simply does not apply. Here is a centrally important statement by C. G. Jung's colleague, Erich Neumann:

Ego-consciousness is the distinguishing characteristic of the human species. It is one of the most significant instruments or organs that enabled human beings to develop a nearly unlimited capacity for adaptation to every possible earthly environment in contrast to most other living creatures. An essential achievement of the ego-consciousness has been the construction of the picture of a so-called objective "real outer world."[2]

Neumann notes that most living creatures form a unity with their specific environments, and that if the environment is disturbed significantly, the species may well die. He concludes, "Thus, non-human creatures are largely field-determined and unfree."[3] Here, freedom is seen in relation to one's environment. Humans may be able to create portable physical environments in submarines and space stations or at the frozen poles of the earth, but rigid psychological environments still trap most of us in one circumstance or another.

The importance of our ego-consciousness in relation to powerful psychological fields is that *only if something comes to awareness is there any possibility at all to change it*. The very measure of our freedom is our ability to perceive contradictions and to change our way of living based on facts. By means of the extraordinary development of our cerebral cortex, we have the capacity of imaging reality. This has enabled us to distance ourselves from the immediacy of animal awareness, to evaluate options, and to choose our action.

It is known that humans can psychologically prevent themselves from being able to see things they do not believe are there. If a zebra were somehow to wind up at the North Pole, for example, human observers might simply refuse to believe they saw it. Thus, the very perception involved in the process of imaging reality also requires openness; where we are closed, we are "field-determined and unfree."

In addition, there are many ways in which we humans sacrifice our freedom to environmental fields, especially cultural fields. In South Africa I was told, "No Zulu would ever get a divorce" and "No Indian would ever get a divorce." The prohibition against divorce is a mighty example of a cultural field, and in certain societies, such rules and others are strongly enforced, culturally speaking. We can recall that the same assumptions were held in our own culture not so long ago. From our present perspective, we can see that they do indeed render individuals "field-determined and unfree."

We also see the controlling effects of psychological fields in mob psychology. Another kind of psychological field is felt in the presence of strong individuals. We call it charisma. Whether we are intimidated or inspired by others, we sacrifice our freedom.

Ideally, we live within some fields, such as the law, by consent and with conscious awareness of what we do. Our consent may be withdrawn, however, if those to whom power is entrusted abuse it. The temptation to abuse power of all sorts is not that different from other controlling fields. It is the field-power of the environment in which the abuse is possible that reduces the real freedom of individuals to live according to wider values. The freedom to abuse power is not really a conscious freedom in the deeper sense of consciousness mentioned above.

In order to be free, we need the best images of reality that we are able to acquire. Where we fail in the task of gaining these images, cultural assumptions take over and we sacrifice our freedom. This quest is by no means limited to physical reality, that is, understanding the nature of the universe. It includes our understanding of ourselves, of the human psyche, and especially of its depth. We need to understand how to perceive when rigid fields are acting upon us and how to gain the strength to choose under such pressures. The field of advertising is an everyday example. It is effective, but we need not succumb to it. Only by continual self-challenge and thoughtful probing of reality can we minimize cultural determinants and maximize our freedom.

The Unus Mundus

Is nature one? Are we part of nature? Many people have believed, and they would confidently assert that they have known that they live in a world with two major acts of creation. The first is the creation of the material world, including its plants and animals, and the second is the special creation of humans: "The Lord God formed man from the dust of the earth; he breathed into his nostrils the breath of life, and man became a living being" (Genesis 2:7). In the same vein, many might say,

"We are *in* the world, but not *of* the world." Is it so? Is human life a special creation, or are we a part of nature?

Any physicist or astronomer will freely accept the word *universe* into a conversation, perhaps without deep awareness of the implications of doing so; for the suffix *uni* denotes something that is "one" or "unified." The same scientist will also speak of the unity of physical laws everywhere throughout the observable cosmos as to space and clear back to the Big Bang in time, and will even marvel at the unity of structure throughout.

However, if we assert that life and consciousness are part of that same unity as well, reductionist scientists balk, for life cannot be accounted for in a rationalistic universe. Nearly seventy years ago, Pierre Teilhard de Chardin correctly argued that the characteristic freedom of living things cannot be derived from atoms as "elementary determinisms," but only from atoms as "elementary freedoms."[4] This argument is outlined in the appendix. But if we exclude life, in the moment we do so, we are assuming that a second, different universe exists together with the first. Then life becomes a special creation, just as in the religious view mentioned above.

If life is indeed a part of the natural order, the currently dominant scientific attitude is in great need of revision, needing to transcend rationalism and become more whole. If the universe includes the possibility of life in a unitary principle, it is nonrational at root. Thus we come to the *unus mundus*.

In her important book *Number and Time*, Jung's colleague Marie-Louise von Franz gives a capsule history of the idea of the *unus mundus*:

Jung used the expression unus mundus *to designate the transcendental unitary reality underlying the dualism of spirit and matter. . . . The expression* unus mundus *originated in medieval*

natural philosophy, where it denoted the timeless, pre-existent,
cosmic plan or antecedent world model, potential in God's mind.
Joannes Scotus Erigena, for instance, describes the process of cre-
ation . . . as "God's seminal power, which flows from a nothing-
ness beyond all being and nonbeing into forms innumerable."[5]

That which unifies spirit and matter is a world of meaning. One
mode in which that meaning operates is synchronicity.

Synchronicity

When seemingly chance events happen to us that exactly reflect our state of mind in an astonishingly meaningful way—
the sorts of things that make us feel that some greater power is
looking after us (or maybe out to get us)—we experience what
Jung called "synchronicity."

A friend of mine was explaining synchronicity to a
group of teenagers during a walk in the woods. "It's as if," he
said, "you were to scoop your hand down to the path at random,
like this, and an arrowhead was there." He reached down and,
to his endless amazement, picked up an arrowhead. He had not
planned this, but was only making an analogy. The arrowhead
was "just" there.

Proponents of standard science, when confronted with
a meaningful coincidence of a physical event with a psychic
state, and when there is no question of either the event's or the
state's causing the other within scientific criteria, would say it
was "merely chance, perhaps an interesting happening, but
science deals only with events that are caused." In fact, even
hard science is riddled with acausal phenomena, the best
known of which is radioactivity.

Radioactive substances such as carbon-14 can be
used in the dating of organic materials from archeological sites

because the "activity" of the material decreases in a known way as its atoms "decay." (In the decay process, carbon-14 atoms become nitrogen-14 atoms that are no longer radioactive and that leak away, since nitrogen is a gas.) The decrease in activity of the whole sample of carbon-14 atoms follows a definite pattern that can be described mathematically, even though the individual atoms are independent of the others. In fact, we can obtain the mathematical form that describes the rate of decline of the activity only by denying that causality has any role in the decay of any single atom. Physicists even call the key to arriving at the mathematical formula the "as-good-as-new-hypothesis." That is, if an atom of the substance has survived to a given moment, it is "as good as new." Its past history has nothing to do with whether it will decay in the next interval of time. Since we have a definite instance in which causality must be denied in arriving at a known, measured law of physics, causality as such cannot be thought of as a universal scientific principle.

A curious fact about synchronicity, which it shares with parapsychological phenomena, is the role of the emotional state of those to whom it occurs. Heightened emotional states, such as we go through when falling in love or experiencing great losses, increase the probability of synchronous events, or at least our awareness of them. It is then that we are closest to the world of meaning, closest to the field.

Such "meaning-events" are generally unique, while scientific validity depends totally on experimental repeatability. It is no wonder, then, that the emotions associated with synchronicity are so ardently avoided in the process of scientific investigation. Although most scientists can discard unique events with equanimity, the fact that they even exist is a perpetual irritation.

The relationship between scientific rationality and the

emotional state that enables us to experience synchronicity is symbolically reflected in the fact that the cerebral cortex, the seat of our ego-consciousness and our rationality, is the main tool of investigative science, while our motivations lie deeper. In *The Man Who Tasted Shapes*, neurologist Richard Cytowic tells us that:

While the cortex contains our model of reality, and analyzes what exists outside ourselves, it is the limbic [interior] brain that determines the salience of that information. . . . Because of this, it is an emotional evaluation, not a reasoned one, that ultimately informs our behavior. [This means that] emotion and mentation not normally accessible to self-awareness have been in charge all along.[6]

The words "mentation not normally accessible to self-awareness" are an oblique reference to kinds of knowledge that do not employ contrasts—what we would call "field-knowledge."

Another point that Cytowic stresses is that humans have not developed ego-consciousness at the expense of emotional development. As he says, "Limbic and cortical circuits co-evolved, and so reason and emotion burgeoned together in tandem."[7] And a standard psychological textbook on the brain says:

In fact, the higher up the evolutionary scale an animal is, the more emotion it can display. Human beings are the most emotional creatures of all, with many highly differentiated emotional expressions and a wide variety of reported emotional experiences.[8]

Because of the many interconnections between the interior brain and the cortex, and the representation and processing of emotions in the cortex, we are aware of at least some of what is going on. The same circumstance also enables us to become emotionally involved with ideas—to become social or religious crusaders, or to feel shame at not living up to some ideal.

And we can also choose on the basis of cognitive value. This is one of the great and enduring themes of literature. Without the distancing that comes from having a cognitive evaluative structure separate from our emotional evaluative structure, we would be forever trapped in animal immediacy.

What goes on in the interior brain is unconscious to us unless a representation of it comes to the cortex. In synchronicity, the field breaks through to our awareness. Do these two statements say the same thing? I believe that they do, that the interior brain is our link to the field in general, and our experienced emotions are its messengers.

When synchronistic phenomena occur, we are impressed by the unity of meaning of the outer physical occurrence with the inner psychic state. These phenomena are numinous, and we generally take them as messages from the "beyond." We need to open our awareness to see them as clear manifestations of the unity behind the disparate natures of the physical and the psychic realms, for they are the only concrete events that show us that link so far.

As we currently know this connection, then, these are intermittent. Are they, perhaps, just one form of a much more general meaning-connection, perhaps joining all events, of which we might be much more aware if we knew how to look? Jung thought that this was at least a possibility, and he called it "acausal orderedness." How far such a principle might reach we cannot yet tell. Sometimes it is said that "there are no accidents," and in line with this is the feeling we have that somewhere there is some kind of cognizance of the smallest detail of everything that happens.

We have already seen one form of acausal orderedness in the example of radioactive decay, given just above. There is a very palpable order in the process, seen in the fact that the mathematical rule that describes the observations satisfies all scientific criteria for accurate description. Might this mean that the atoms somehow are connected to each other, in spite of the fact that this seems scientifically impossible? If they were indeed embedded in such a worldfield as we have been trying to present, the idea is not as absurd as at first appearance.

I believe that we will eventually see that such connections are always there, as material and nonmaterial manifestations of a meaning-event in the field. That is, I believe that, as a planet, we will become ever more aware of the presence of the field that connects all phenomena from beyond or behind, as it were: the worldfield.

Of course, we remain free to insist that it was mere chance all along, but then we actively exclude meaning. The worldfield, however, is a field of meaning. That is, we infer its presence by means of these meaningful connections.

Outer and Inner

So far we have pointed to the worldfield in three ways. The first is what we might call the richness of metaphor, the parallel patterns in nature and our human endeavors. Second, we have considered the nonrational unity of opposites, and third, we have just looked at synchronicity. To try to get a better image of the field, we turn now to a long-held assumption that may turn out to be quite questionable: the distinction of inner and outer.

The inner/outer distinction seems clear and obvious to us, and indeed it is essential to our living. We call something "outer" that is tangible and material, while "inner" refers to the realm of feelings, intuitions, ideas, and images. However, if we are to get back to our roots in the field, we will need some means of breaking down the rigid distinction between these two constructs, and some excellent reasons for doing so.

There is also an added psychological dimension to our quest, for most of us still hope to find ourselves in the realm of universals, those things that apply to everyone, always and everywhere. We feel that there should be some path on which we may not need to stand against odds, but can bask in the sunshine of a general consent. Something maybe—well—*scientific*. Or, failing that, something through which we can find the company of like minds. There is, however, in the total reality, that which demands of us that we be ourselves as individuals at all costs, and in particular that we make up our own minds about things, independent of authority of all kinds, especially cultural images.

This is a paradox, of course, because how can another human convince you to go your own way? Immediately, we have "going your own way" as a universal. In the end, of course, there are indeed universals, or at least some facts and principles that are general enough. There are things that we know together, and that is science at its best.

Paradoxes will illumine our way. As we continue our journey through this book, I hope to give you reason enough to consider some out-of-the-way notions. All this introduction is by way of saying that I am about to propose something unusual, to say the least, as another way to boggle ourselves into seeing through the fog of our contrasts.

A Metaphor for the Field

Cytowic's book *The Man Who Tasted Shapes* is about synesthesia, a phenomenon that affects about one in a hundred thousand of us. Those who are affected by it experience what to most of us is one sense, such as taste, as what to most of us is another, such as touch, as does the title character of the book. To other synesthetes, particular sounds may produce particular visual images and colors. A symphony may produce a whole inner "light show." Smells may produce colors, too, and so forth. These responses are not at all "what you would think" they would be if you considered them in symbolic terms; the intellect has nothing to do with it. The responses are concrete, specific, and repeatable, so that, for instance, you can remember a name by its particular color.

However, the point for us is that Cytowic's research into synesthesia showed that it is a "union of the senses," and that all of us have it. To most of us, it is unconscious. We sort out the senses before becoming aware of them. If you think about it as follows, you can see that it must be so.

In the simplest organisms, there is just a generalized stimulus/response phenomenon. The stimulus could be contact (later to become the sense of touch), light or heat (seeing, sensations), chemical (taste and smell), vibration (hearing). But the simplest organisms do not possess the organic equipment to differentiate them. A stimulus brings a response. And even other organisms, more complex but not as complex as humans, probably do not have the images of the senses in a reflective area of their brains, so that they can say, "Ah, that is a smell."

In evolution, organisms gradually develop sensitive organs that become more specific for the stimuli that most occur, but still the senses are united in the pure experience of the environment. The senses inform each other of the totality being experienced.

If we are to have even the concept of an object, our brain must be able to correlate all the different sensory information about it. If you have a friend put some objects into a bag without your seeing them, you can put in your hand and use your other senses to describe them. Size, shape, textures, and heft can be used, perhaps even hearing, if there is something that rattles when you shake it. The point is that our senses are correlated, and the web of images from the different senses is evaluated for something like consistency or familiarity even prior to our being aware that the evaluation is occurring.

But what if the senses were all mixed, as they in fact are in the interior brain? We would experience only an unintelligible jumble of sensations. Our cortex sorts them out; there are specific regions for the images of each. But in the interior brain there is only the experience of the object. *In a sense, we have created the different senses in our awareness of them.* Perhaps some "senses" are left below our awareness because we have not yet evolved to the point of comprehending them. The knowledge that "intuitives" bring to us could well be of such a kind.

That is the metaphor of what the field is like as to outer and inner. *Perhaps inner and outer are incomprehensibly mixed in our total experience*, and we effectively *create* them as separate aspects for our conscious awareness, because without separating them we could not function. In any case, without separating them we could not even "stand back" and look at them as separate, and we would be relatively helpless.

We know through the psychological phenomenon of projection that we meet ourselves in the people and things around us, but that is just one aspect of the field behind the inner-outer duality. There are other hints, even in science, that things are not as neatly divided into outer and inner as they appear.

The outer realm, though it is the realm of matter, is full of nonmaterial contradictions. For instance, our concepts of space and time, which retain much mystery, are included in the material realm by physicists. Using ideas within the physics of relativity, it is possible to argue that there really is no such thing as space and time; the preeminent cosmologist John Archibald Wheeler has said just that.[9] This is not to deny what we consider our everyday experiences of real measurable space and time; it is just that things are not nearly as simple as they seem. We have not only physics to thank for that; but if we are honest, we must face the fact that we have other experiences in which the distinction between inner and outer is quite arbitrary, and these are by no means limited to parapsychological experiments, though they do include them.[10]

As we are learning, the field is creative, active, encompassing, and nurturing. These are, of course, divine attributes. It not only connects opposites, but does so in the context of meaning. As Jung said in his "Answer to Job":

Whatever human wholeness, or the self, may mean per se, empirically it is an image of the goal of life spontaneously produced by the unconscious, regardless of the wishes and fears of the conscious mind. It stands for the goal of human totality, for the realization of our wholeness and individuality with or without the consent of our will. The dynamic of this process is instinct, which ensures that everything which belongs to an individual's life shall enter into it.[11]

Although this statement goes beyond our usual idea of instinct, it is still a clear image of the field as that which brings to us that which we need for wholeness, including, and probably especially, our problems. In those instances where we exclaim, "I didn't need this to happen now," we are most likely dead wrong.

One pair of opposites mentioned above is spirit/matter. Jung made one of his most quoted statements with regard to these. In it he points out how spirit and matter are visible to us because they are part of the contents of our conscious thought. However, because of the limitation of our conscious thought and its contents, spirit and matter transcend them.

Matter and spirit both appear in the psychic realm as distinctive qualities of conscious contents. The ultimate nature of both is transcendental, that is, irrepresentable, since the psyche and its contents is the only reality which is given to us without a medium.[12]

Much of the attitude of the present author is colored by the suggestion of Pierre Teilhard de Chardin that "the stuff of the universe is spirit-matter." In the present model, that "stuff" is "field-stuff," which appears to us in either of its inherent but hidden aspects as spirit or as matter, according to circumstances, just as the electron appears in either of its inherent aspects as a wave or as a particle.

We humans have struggled mightily to achieve knowledge and the autonomy/adaptability/power that knowledge brings. We have indeed worshipped knowledge as a savior. Now we are learning that a pure focus on knowledge is gradually diluting our humanity. Here is another of the pairs of opposites continually involved in the trade-off of mutually exclusive values. In the history of consciousness, knowledge is indeed a savior, but without humanity, we are as lost as we would be without knowledge; humanity is also a savior. We need both opposites; we need wholeness.

As humans, we want to use the best of both our mind and our heart—the best of science and of religion or spirituality, or whatever word you prefer. We now possess sufficient evidence to give concrete standing to the worldfield, even scientifically, but it will require of us more than just the openness to new phenomena within a known framework. We must be ready to revise fundamental conceptions of reality. Neumann prepares us for this enterprise with the following:

Ego-consciousness represents a specifically restricted field of knowledge in which the world-continuum [or worldfield] is broken up into constituent parts. But we must not say, "into its own constituent parts. . . ."[13]

That is, the cosmos yields answers to our probing questions by means of the methods of science, but the concepts that we derive by such means are only one way of breaking the cosmos into understandable pieces.

In this sense, the worldfield is endlessly creative, for it can respond to our hearts' desires without revealing its ultimate nature. Another way of putting it is that it is endlessly and boundlessly *free*.

CHAPTER TWO

The Transformation of Science

If simple and perfect laws uniquely rule the universe, should not pure thought be capable of uncovering this perfect set of laws without having to lean on the crutches of tediously assembled observations?
—Martin Schwarzschild
The Structure and Evolution of the Stars

Four or five centuries ago, educated Europeans generally believed that the earth was the center of the universe, and that the sun, moon, planets, and stars were attached to crystal spheres. These spheres were rigid and transparent so that they could "hold up" the celestial bodies and still give them their observed motions through the sky as the spheres turned on unseen bearings. Observation was still so crude that it was possible to imagine that the universe "above" the earth was perfect, although it was getting to the point that more and more crystal spheres—several for each planet—were needed to account for variations in the motions of the planets.

This not-so-ancient picture of the planetary system has often been cited to show what changes have occurred in the way in which we think of the universe. I want to make a

different point. *What would our life be like if scientific exploration had demonstrated that the crystal sphere conception was
true?* The point will be more potent if I paint a picture of the
model in the present tense.

Try to put yourself, with scientific certainty, into the
picture. Somewhere there *are* great mechanical supports with
immense crystal gears, turning majestically, moving the planets
in their paths, forward and backwards among the images of the
more distant stars. All the stars are at the same fixed distance
from the earth on the greatest sphere of all, turning around the
earth-anchor once each day. The universe is a great closed box.

What would be the theology of such a case? Again, try
to bring it into the present for yourself. We would know with
scientific certainty that the earth *is* the center, the focus of all
of God's attention, with this vast construction for our benefit,
enjoyment, wonder. The theology of the fifteenth century will
do, unchanged.

Would there even *be* scientific exploration? If we had
come to the point of sending rockets higher and higher, we
would, first of all, be blaspheming, by putting God to the test,
but if we still dared, what would happen when one of the rockets bounced back from the first crystal sphere?

This play could be continued for quite some time, with
all kinds of imaginary consequences.

The point is that our everyday lives are intimately
bound up with our view of the universe. In fact, they are bound
up with the whole of science, since, for starters, science gives
birth to technology. Scientific exploration changes our theology
for better or worse. But can good theology conflict with good
science? Can good science expose bad theology?

We may be free to believe anything we want to, but
would we still be so free if, as we hypothesized above, scientific exploration had demonstrated that the crystal sphere idea

was true? Good science actually protects our right to believe the absurd, for its primary criterion is evidence, not authority. We would no longer be able to maintain freedom of belief under the circumstances pictured above, in which science verified a fixed theology.

While it is true that "mainstream" theology has evolved tremendously under the impact of scientific discoveries, we should note that in societies where education is prevalent, everyday life has assimilated these discoveries quite apart from theology.

Mechanics and Mystics

If I have given the impression that science is some sort of infallible guide for every aspect of life, I am going to begin now to correct that impression. Scientists are just as likely as anyone else to stick to the status quo and not budge when new insights sail into view.

The evolution of our scientific worldview has not been a smooth, steady progression. Just as life evolved by fits and starts, there have been long periods in which the generally held worldview has been quite stable, but then the prevailing images were turned upside down by deep transformations. I am going to be pointing to three tremendous shifts, the first of which is the Western birth of science itself.

Each of these revolutionary shifts highlights a pair of scientists, but the issue is essentially the same in each case: one of the scientists is a "mechanic," which is to say an experimentalist, while the other is a "mystic," that is, a theoretician. The inspiration for these designations comes from Carl Sagan's book *Cosmos*. First, the mechanics:

The key to the revolution [the birth of science] was the hand.
Some of the brilliant Ionian thinkers were the sons of sailors and
farmers and weavers. They were accustomed to poking and fix-
ing, unlike the priests and scribes of other nations, who, raised
in luxury, were reluctant to dirty their hands.[1]

In the early sixth century B.C.E., Thales, having examined Babylonian records, correctly predicted the eclipse of the sun that occurred in 585 B.C.E. The very idea behind the prediction, that there might be patterns in nature, was revolutionary. Prior to that time, eclipses were thought to occur at the instance of a god, to warn humanity that things were not on track. In order to even think of predicting an eclipse, Thales had to stand aloof from the prevailing theology.

The Ionians were not wealthy, at least at first, but trade was expanding through their area. In Athens, the merchants were wealthy and disdained not only manual work, but crafts as well, as has been the case in many cultures. As Xenophon, an Athenian aristocrat, put it, "What are called the mechanical arts carry a social stigma and are rightly dishonored in our cities."[2] Craftspersons, of course, made the instruments through which the next great advances in science were accomplished, and that technical skill has made the difference between experimentalists and theoreticians time and time again.

Shortly after Thales made his initial steps, an opposing view arose virtually at his doorstep, in the person of Pythagoras. As Sagan puts it:

Many of the Ionians believed the underlying harmony of the
universe to be accessible through observation and experiment.
. . . However, Pythagoras employed a very different method. He
taught that the laws of Nature could be deduced by pure

*thought. He and his followers were not fundamentally experi-
mentalists. They were mathematicians. And they were thor-
oughgoing mystics.*[3]

Sagan's comment that mathematics and mysticism go hand in
hand is amazingly insightful, though this kind of mysticism has
nothing to do with that religious mysticism that denotes the direct perception of the ineffable. Most mathematicians believe
in a kind of Platonic world of absolute certainty, absolute ide-
alism, which does indeed reflect a kind of mysticism. While
there is no question about the fact that mathematical descrip-
tions of physical reality are potent, the best minds have always
perceived that the connection between mathematics and observed physical reality is indeed a mystery. Sagan himself was
intoxicated with mathematics, in part because he believed in a
rationally knowable world:

*In the recognition by Pythagoras and Plato that the Cosmos is
knowable, that there is a mathematical underpinning to nature,
they greatly advanced the cause of science.*[4]

Martin Schwarzschild's question in the epigraph at the beginning of this chapter also reflects this view.[5] Today, we would
have to say that the notion that there is a mathematical underpinning to nature is acceptable as far as it goes. As a description of general processes, mathematics does indeed apply to
the universe, but it remains no better in its descriptive powers
than our ability to conceptualize the cosmos, for the little symbols that we put into equations may not represent precisely
what we think they do. That is, the math may be correct, but
we still may be doing inadequate physics.

The cosmos is indeed knowable, but only partially,
only approximately. Theoreticians, our mystics, simply assume

unconsciously that we know physical reality directly and can ultimately know it fully. Neither of these assumptions can be sustained.

The real success of theory has encouraged our belief in an ideal realm such as was at the heart of Plato's thought. This belief had to be played out until it ran into compelling reasons to abandon it. Those reasons have now appeared.

It has taken 2500 years, but now we know that *the rational structure devised by human thought is only one way of perceiving the world.* The unconscious assumption in Schwarzchild's epigraph is that the laws are not only to be "simple and perfect" but in the human rational mode as well. Our concepts of things are precisely that: *our* concepts of things, rather than the *things themselves.* Once again our hubris has misled us.

The Ionian awakening has been seen as rationalism emerging to combat mysticism, but it is probably more accurate to say that it arose from naturalism combating the supernatural. Rationalism and mysticism both fall into the province of the Pythagoreans, whose beliefs were virtually as mystical as the religions of Greece. They did make a scientific contribution in that they felt, along with the school of Thales, that the universe can be known, and their attitude released a lot of human energy to search for knowledge about the universe. The battle concerned the means of knowing it: observation for the mechanics, pure thought for the mystics. As Schwarzschild's comment shows, the battle is still with us.

Naturalism was suppressed after flourishing for less than two centuries. The mercantile tradition of Ionia was bearing fruit, and with their new wealth, the Ionians became interested in spiritualism of the Pythagorean sort. They also became slave owners, and one of the attributes of the slave-owning mindset is authoritarianism, which plagues standard science to this day, especially in the theoretical camp.

The birth of Christianity reinforced the authoritarianism of spiritualism. Curiously, it did so through the figure of the pre-Christian philosopher Aristotle, with devastating consequences for the progress of science. Aristotle's teachings exerted such a powerful grip on the scientific mind that to reach our next major transformation we have to jump forward over two thousand years from Thales' time.

Our next mechanic was Johannes Kepler, though he began as a mystic's mystic, and it took him a long time to abandon that position. And our mystic was Galileo—a characterization that may surprise many, for Galileo made powerful use of observation. He employed his telescope in combating the authoritarianism of Aristotle and the church. He is also said to have conducted the famous experiment of dropping balls of two different weights from the leaning tower of Pisa, showing that they fall at the same rate and hit the ground at the same instant. It is quite uncertain, however, whether he actually did this.

The fact is that he would not have felt that he needed to actually perform the experiment, since, through what are now called "thought experiments," he could show that it would be unreasonable for the balls to do anything else but hit the ground simultaneously, and so he earns his classification with the mystics. Galileo's invention of these thought experiments contributed greatly to the development of physics. One can do a great deal with them.

One such experiment consists in imagining whether, if you were to drop a stone next to the mast of a ship that is moving (at constant speed), it will fall next to the foot of the mast as it does when the ship is not moving. Aristotle said that the stone would fall behind the mast, since the ship had moved while the stone was falling, but Galileo argued (correctly) that, since the stone was moving horizontally with the ship when it was dropped, it would retain that motion and fall next to the foot of the mast, just as it does when the ship is at rest. In his *Dialogue Concerning the Two Chief World Systems*, Galileo's protagonist, Salviati, is debating this very experiment with an Aristotelian, Simplicio. After a while, it becomes apparent that Salviati (Galileo) has not actually made these tests.

Simplicio: *So you have not made a hundred tests, or even one? And yet you so freely declare it to be certain? . . .*

Salviati: *Without experiment, I am sure that the effect will happen as I tell you, because it must happen that way. . . .*[6]

The clincher comes later, while they are debating the question of whether the earth moves:

Salviati: *Nor can I ever sufficiently admire the outstanding acumen of those who have taken hold of this opinion [of Pythagoras that the earth moves] and accepted it as true; they have through sheer force of intellect done such violence to their own senses as to prefer what reason told them over that which sense experience plainly showed them to the contrary.*[7]

This makes it clear that, while observable events certainly enter the discussion, it is reason, not observation, that finally determines what is occurring. This is a mystic speaking.

Galileo's reason for arguing that the earth moves had nothing to do with observation. He saw that the Copernican view that the sun was the center of the universe and that earth was one of its planets made for a more simple system. For that reason alone, he believed the Copernican system was more likely to be true. Galileo was tried for heresy by the church for claiming that the earth moves, contrary to scriptures such as Psalms 93:1 and 96:10, which say, "The world is established; it shall never be moved."

Because the earth does move, and because of many other conflicts between observation and scripture, we have come to see that scriptures are symbolic. We have gradually learned to understand passages such as those in the psalms just cited as referring to the formation of an inner, stable, religious foundation.

While reason is powerful in ferreting out that which is unreasonable, in the end it can never predict all possible new phenomena. For that, we need the mechanics, the observers, the experimenters.

I said above that Kepler began as a mystic's mystic. In fact, his primary inspiration was the Pythagorean idea of the "harmony of the spheres," or a cosmic music played out by the planets. He felt certain that there was a link between the five gaps that separated the six known planets and the five "regular geometric solids" (the tetrahedron, the cube, the octahedron, the icosahedron, and the dodecahedron). This conviction on his part arose out of his belief that numbers are divine (also a Pythagorean concept). To prove that the geometric figures somehow determined the spacing of the planets, he sought out the most accurate observations he could obtain.

Eventually, Kepler came into possession of Tycho Brahe's observations of the planets, which were the most precise measurements of which the human eye is capable without the aid of a telescope. Their accuracy is about one-sixtieth of a degree, also known as a "minute of arc." For years, Kepler struggled to fit various circular orbits to the data, to no avail.

The orbit of Mars, in particular, would not fit any circular scheme, and he had to admit to himself that his great idea did not work. All the same, he continued his attempt to determine a circular orbit that would fit Brahe's data for Mars. The idea that heavenly perfection demanded circular orbits was another Pythagorean doctrine, which had been perpetuated for two millennia as self-evident. Kepler worked until he had found a circle that would work, if he could bring himself to believe that Tycho's observations had been incorrect by only eight minutes of arc.

At this point, Kepler's integrity held; he knew that the observations were much better than that. Thus, Kepler became the first modern scientist of importance to give priority to observation over ideas in giving up cherished mystical ideals. The fact that he went on to discover that orbits of the planets are ellipses, not circles, is of less importance than that he made the shift to trusting observation. The mechanics were regaining their place in science.

The twentieth century has witnessed a third great struggle of the mystics and mechanics. Both have had triumphs, because the roles of theory and experimentation are drawing closer together, ever more intertwined, and also because our models of physical reality come ever closer to the real.

Because of the impact of "external" fact, we have come to an understanding of the symbolic nature of inspired writings. Now, as we saw in chapter 1, it is time to begin to understand that nature, too, cannot quite be taken literally. We must understand nature symbolically as well.

In this third struggle, our mystic is Einstein, and Niels Bohr is our mechanic. In this case, the shift in our thinking is so profound that the issue will occupy the whole next chapter, but we can at least introduce it here, as it rounds out the story of mystics and mechanics.

When, in 1919, observations of shifts in the apparent positions of stars near the eclipsed sun agreed with his prediction of the way gravitational attraction acts on starlight, Einstein was said to remark, in the best mystical tradition, "If the results had not been so, I would have been sorry for the good Lord; the theory is correct!"

Einstein's relativity theory was founded on principles of symmetry, and his approach to knowledge in this regard has borne fruit well beyond the experimental confirmation of relativity itself. Symmetry principles have served as guides to experimental discoveries of numerous subatomic particles, for instance. If we have a piece of a puzzle, theoretical considerations can often help fill in the picture. What they cannot do is predict something completely new.

Bohr always argued from facts, or from the nature of measurement, even when the facts led him into nonrational realms. His first major contribution to our understanding of reality was his model of the atom, with the electrons in orbits around the nucleus. Even at the time, the model of the electron as a particle made it impossible for an electron to do any such thing; particle-like electrons in such orbits must radiate energy and matter must collapse. However, Bohr said to himself that since matter *is* stable, something like an orbit must be the case. Much later, we realized that electrons in atoms are in their wave state, and that makes stability possible. Thus, we now know that the picture of electrons as particles in orbit is wrong, though it still fills our science books, and we see it carved in stone on the facades of science buildings.

Einstein, however, held out against the nonrational to the end of his days, in defiance of facts. In fairness, it must be said that the facts were conclusively confirmed only after his death, but they were available to him during his lifetime. These facts concerned the dual nature of electrons that we have already seen in the model in chapter 1, and they deny the very structure of the logic in which we have trusted these two thousand years. That is, *rationalistic logic occupies an ideal world; it is the tool of mystics.* And that is where we will leave the metaphor of mechanics and mystics for now.

The Fall of Rationalism

Physics is the foundation of the sciences. Not only chemistry and other "hard" sciences, but the biological sciences as well spring from physics. The nature of physical reality, as discovered by physics and its cosmological cousin, astronomy, applies throughout all scientific study. If physics gives rise to an unduly limited worldview, as is presently the case in standard science, the defects are transmitted into the whole of science and beyond, including psychology, philosophy, and religion, for these fields hold worldviews that are dependent on our understanding of physics, as we saw in the case of Galileo.

At present, the scientific worldview is undergoing a radical change, from rationalism, also known in science as reductionism, to a new foundation, a more comprehensive worldview known as complementarity (which will be described in the next chapter). Strictly speaking, rationalism applies to concepts and logical constructs, while reductionism applies to phenomena. The assumption (applicable to both ideas and phenomena) that is undergoing transformation is that wholes are ultimately made up of parts that are simple, clear, distinct, and objective.

Physical science is now confronted with phenomena

that reductionism cannot digest—nonrational phenomena which cannot be assimilated into the old worldview, but which for just that reason point to the greater wholeness of the view to come. The worldview of complementarity promises to explain problems well beyond the sciences, having an impact on philosophy, theology, and the social and political sciences, though all this will take some time. The issues are numerous and complex, and if transformation is a long and difficult process in individuals, it is much more so where groups are concerned.

No less than for the ancients, our current worldview is our current myth. That is, our images of reality, even those suggested by mathematics, are mythic projections, which is to say that the only images that are available to us for conceptualizing reality are those presented from within the human psyche.[8]

We can justifiably describe science as a powerful human enterprise, but our emphasis should be on the word "human." It is humans who engage in science, and the human psyche resists a change of worldview. In principle, the scientific attitude is one that interprets phenomena to discover the true nature of physical reality, whatever that may be. In practice, though, scientists are likely to be as power-conscious and territorial as anyone else.

Scientists have been inspired by reductionism, with its promise of a rational and explicable world. Energized by this goal, they have harnessed tremendous powers of nature and have acquired insights and knowledge completely unimaginable in advance. Their work shows its validity partly through the effectiveness of the technology that is its offspring. They have been mistaken, however, in assuming that the validity of their work depends on the validity of the rationalistic-reductionistic worldview that was their inspiration. They hold on to the worldview because they fear that their work would be invalidated if their worldview were to change. It should, however, be a liberation to let go of a departing mindset.

For example, the scientific worldview once included Newton's idea of absolute space and time. When this idea disintegrated under the power of Einstein's relativity theory, many physicists feared that the whole scientific edifice was threatened with collapse. They either ignored Einstein's theory or attempted to fight it.

The sciences of mechanics and thermodynamics, for instance, work very well within the Newtonian view of time and space, and the validity of these scientific fields remains intact today. We can now see that their validity did not depend on the Newtonian worldview at all, but only on the fact that they work.

It is the same with reductionism, now threatened by complementarity, for scientists tend to think that the validity of their work depends on the validity of mathematical logic, which is a part of the rationalistic worldview.

The foundation stone of mathematical logic is the proposition that any logical statement must be either true or false, with no middle ground for partial truth or falsity. Another proposition says that if a single logical statement and its negation are both simultaneously true, then all logical statements are automatically true, and nothing can then be decided. Complementarity threatens both of these propositions, as applicable to physical reality, on the basis of observations of physical phenomena, as exemplified by the fact that we observe a single electron behaving both as a particle and as a wave. The logical propositions are true in logic, but ultimately not in the physical world—for the world turns out to be quite independent of the logic in question.

Logic maximizes contrasts between cases; in fact it makes contrasts absolute, as can be seen in the foundational proposition given just above, that any logical statement must be either true or false. Logic leaves no middle ground between what it calls truth and falsity, no gray shadow area. What science wants to discover, however, is what the cosmos at root actually is like; and it is only in limited circumstances that the cosmos appears to obey the propositions of logic.

Changing Worldviews

It is a virtue (and not only in science) to be skeptical, not giving our credence cheaply. Skepticism reflects a real concern for truth. Yet it is also a virtue to be open to new ideas and facts, not using our skepticism to form a psychological defense around a system of beliefs. Skepticism and openness push in opposite directions, but we can easily see that if one goes too far in skepticism, then openness would be the cure, and vice versa. Together, then, they form a whole, which does not solve the question rationally as to which attitude is most needed in a given situation, but leaves that question up to the consciousness of the individual concerned.

Scientific objectivity, part of the rationalistic-reductionistic worldview, is a myth. In fact, any worldview concerning physical reality is essentially mythic in nature. The word mythic does not imply untruth or fantastic invention. It means merely that since the reality in itself cannot be known, we must express what we know of it symbolically. A myth is that which tells a certain kind of nonrational truth as it can best be told. Besides, processes in the human psyche often require images that cross the borderline of the fantastic in order to do justice to reality, as we saw in the case of Bohr's atom, above. The realm of physical science has seemed to be the very opposite of the fantastic, yet it has always partaken of the fantastic to some degree. New and surprising powers in nature continually come to light. Though it has been the conscious intent of science to demythologize nature, it remains eternally true that our current worldview is our current myth.

As a serpent sheds skins, Western culture has shed its images of the cosmos time after time, yet a skin always remains a skin. This means that any worldview that succeeds the present worldview of standard physics will be no less mythic, though it will indeed be more effective in the interpretation of nature. As with the new skin of the serpent, the new skin of the coming worldview is growing underneath the old, and the old skin cannot be safely shed until that new worldview reaches a state of maturity. Then, for a while, the new skin will display a beautiful and powerful animal, but its aging will be inevitable.

The present myth, now well past its days of strength, is that of the "clockwork" universe—the machinelike universe of reductionism. This myth has come to the fullness of its yield of meaning with the advent of the image and reality of the computer. The signs of the new skin growing under the old are seen in American popular culture in such "human" computers as Hal in the film *2001, A Space Odyssey* and Data in the television series *Star Trek, the Next Generation.* These tales explore the implications of computers with feelings and motivations. They attempt to bridge the gap between people and machines from the side of the machine. True, these popular screen fictions still promote the idea that humans are merely complex machines, which is part of the worldview of the clockwork universe. Yet their acceptance of the notion that the gap *can* be bridged is evidence of the new worldview growing underneath the old.

In the same century that we began to feel threatened by the possibility that we are only machines, and that computers will ultimately reproduce everything human—imagination, feelings, and all—science itself came up against stronger and stronger evidence of the ultimate nonrationality of the elementary pieces of which the material universe is composed. This new development provides a wholly different basis for the spiritual possibilities of humanity and the new forms into which humanity will evolve.

To summarize, the historic and prevailing attitude of standard physics is most clearly represented in the two words *reductionism* (rationalism) and *objectivity.* As absolutes, both of these ideals have failed, though the failure has not yet been recognized by standard science.

Rationalism is the assumption that both our concepts and the world itself are made up of elements that are ultimately simple, clear, and distinct, and that if contradictions arise, there can be only one cause: error. Alfred North Whitehead stated this position with great force.[9]

This is the psychological milieu that we assimilated as our elementary school teachers graded our arithmetic papers. There are only two kinds of answers, right and wrong, and there is only one right answer! Of course, in elementary arithmetic and algebra, this is true, but we have tended to generalize this attitude to other human doings.

Objectivity, the ideal that we ought to be able to know what things are and how they behave in themselves, was first challenged by Kant in the late-eighteenth century when he argued that we cannot know things in themselves because the concepts by means of which we know things are our concepts, the framework of our own understanding. We thus have no way to guarantee that these concepts actually apply to the objects of our study. Everything we know has some subjective element, something attributed to it in an unperceived manner from within our own psyche. Therefore, absolute objectivity is impossible.

For two centuries, science has ignored this warning because of its unfounded assumption that our reason should be able to see why things must be exactly as they are. That is, pure reason should be able to come up with a description of the world and the physical reality that we do in fact see, and should be able to direct experiments that would confirm that view and never contradict it. As we have seen, this belief in the power of pure reason was succinctly expressed by Martin Schwarzschild in the statement quoted in the epigraph to this chapter. On this simple question of whether we must observe in order to know hangs the fate of the worldview of standard physics. In fact we must, for *rational thought would not, could not, have led us to what we now know to be the nonrational character of physical reality.* We first must see a phenomenon. Then we can describe it, i.e., put it into concepts, and try to explain it.

What we observe, and agree with others as to what we are observing, is what we call factual. The word "fact" evokes contradictory feelings in people. For some it denotes the very bits or pieces of a cold and rationalistic cosmos, and it brings forth a response of distrust and disgust. Perhaps this is because people have experienced lies being presented as fact by governments intent on power and control, or because the law is so often pursued with regard to fact rather than for the end of true justice.

On the other hand, there is a true shape of reality for us to discover, and we speak of "facing the facts" as a central component of responsible, effective living. We have a deep need to align ourselves with what truly is the case as closely as we are able. For many of us the most important facts concern the reality of love rather than the mere disposition of material objects in time and space, the facts that would matter most in a court proceeding.

If we did live in an objective and rationalistic universe, facts could indeed be reduced to something cold and hard, and the influence of the observer could be nullified. However, in such a universe, life is actually impossible. (See Appendix: "The Anthropic Principle.") In the emerging worldview, the human element is not eradicated, because the wholeness of reality includes human consciousness.

Effective Truth

All facts share the "flaw" of having a subjective component, but they are nevertheless effective enough for us to get on with living. In this view, we let go of absolute objectivity and accept a *relative* objectivity grounded in our agreement as to what is observed. As we have seen, fact guides the formation of theory, and fact also eventually overrides theory and changes it into something new.

Theoretical standard physics has continued to believe in its own objectivity. It has taken refuge in the notion that if the cosmos is rational, pure thought might yet show us that what we observe cannot be other than as we see it.

In this century, however, rationalism has foundered, since in quantum physics we now possess facts for which there is no possible rational interpretation. As we saw in chapter 1, the elementary entities of which the physical world is made exhibit properties that are logically contradictory. The properties popularly known as "wave" and "particle" stand more precisely for continuity and discontinuity, which makes their logical contradiction evident.

There is a difficulty in referring to elementary entities such as electrons and photons. The names of each imply the particle aspect, which biases the understanding toward that interpretation. On the other hand, to always say "elementary entities" is rather stiff. I will use the terms "electron" and "photon" to refer to them as *wholes*, implicitly including the fact that either of these can manifest itself as particle or wave, depending on the circumstances. Electrons and photons will be the main examples of things that are both waves and particles as we continue. To be sure, these entities are seen as one or the other only at a given instant; but each is supposedly simple, and rationally should not possess the capacity for showing logically contradictory qualities. It would be too much to describe the definitive experiments of the last few years, but in the cases of both photons and electrons, single particles have been made to show their wave properties by taking two different and highly separated paths simultaneously, a behavior impossible for particles by any rational definition. The wholeness or integrity of the particles is effectively maintained by means of the contradictory property, its wave nature.

If elementary entities are elementary wholes that embrace opposite aspects, then that which emerges in evolution should retain the property of wholeness in the same sense. Indeed that is what we find when we see things inclusively, including our vision of ourselves.

Physicists mostly stress the particle aspect of things because it is convenient, and because it gives an aura of clarity. Thus they pass over the reality of the wave state of electrons and other traditional particles. An exception was Erwin Schrödinger, who felt that the wave/particle dilemma should be resolved in favor of waves.[10] We now know, however, that it cannot be resolved at all. Resolving the dilemma is still a rationalistic aim.

A great many problems can be solved using reductive techniques, especially in science. But even in science there are cases where those techniques lead as much away from the truth as toward it, and in some cases they are absolutely misleading.

Effective truth, in science as well as in our lives, is always about *wholes*.

CHAPTER THREE

The Rise of Complementarity

Evidence conclusive, either way.
—*Kenneth Patchen,* Sleepers Awake

The mythic basis of science is changing. The ideals of a fully rational world-system and absolute objectivity are not merely under threat, they are no longer tenable at all. Scientists prefer to use words such as *model* and *paradigm* rather than *myth* and *metaphor* in describing the basis of the scientific view; yet these words all say the same thing. *Model* and *paradigm* sound less mysterious, more scientific. Nevertheless, as we continue our quest for understanding, even scientific understanding, we must be open to the inclusion of mystery.

The newer myth of our time, notwithstanding the fact that it is very ancient, is wholeness. This wholeness comes in the form of the unity of opposites, of which much has already been said in earlier chapters. Human wholeness unites our heart with our mind, our conscious and unconscious sides, ourselves with others, and our physical and spiritual health concerns, to name just four pairs of opposites. In science, wholeness also takes several forms, including the connectedness and disconnectedness that we call the wave and particle aspects of things, the observer and the observed, and also unites the realm of meaning to what has been merely cold knowledge.

Given the human suffering that has accompanied the enmity of science and religion, this move toward wholeness is indeed a healing possibility. If we can cut away the images that have held us in thrall on one side or other of the divide between them, it will be highly liberating as well.

No worldview holds, or can hold, a final answer, so we cannot expect that the shift will give us "the truth at last." At best, it is a healing of the times, for the time being. It is a growing in an eternal unfolding process in the universe. In affording a more adequate vision of the nature of physical reality, and of spiritual reality as well, the emerging myth gives us plenty to work with for a long time to come. At this stage, the vision we are headed toward is nothing less than the unity of the great opposites, spirit and matter.

The single word that most clearly characterizes the new model, as it has taken shape in science, is *complementarity*, the nonrational unity of opposites. Physicist Niels Bohr, who first applied the term in physics, saw the implications of this view deeply, in that the concept applies very generally beyond physics. When an award he had received required him to have a coat-of-arms, the motto he adopted was: "Opposites are complementary."[1] Bohr first used complementarity successfully in building a tentative model of the atom by consciously including contradictory concepts. That is, while the concepts of wave and particle logically contradict each other, both are needed, and complement each other, in describing the nature of electrons and photons. Thus opposites are *both* contradictory *and* complementary. This statement reflects the experimental facts. As we saw at the end of chapter 2, in experiments since 1991, single photons and single electrons have been shown definitively to exhibit both logically contradictory aspects, wave and particle. These experimental results point to a unity behind the opposites, which we named the worldfield (chapter 1).

An excellent general definition of complementarity has been given by Edward Teller:

The idea of complementarity is that in order to describe a situation you have to use (at least on certain occasions) two mutually exclusive approaches. If you omit either, the description is incomplete. Both must be used. Because they are mutually exclusive, it is necessary to adjust the two approaches in a manner that is by no means obvious.[2]

Actually, the mild expression "by no means obvious" turns out to mean that there is no rational solution to the problem of how to adjust the two approaches, and thus that we, the observers, are called upon to enter the situation with choice and intuition. That is how the universe draws us into its own being as participants.

Previously, we said that the electron or photon can show both aspects (both wave and particle behavior), but that needs to be qualified. At any single instant, one of these entities can exhibit only one aspect or the other. That is, in the realm of our perceptions, it is either wave or particle, but not both at the same time. This means that the wholeness of the electron or of the photon is a pre-perceptual unity. Wave and particle are the observable forms of the electron or photon, the only modes in which we can perceive them at all. The wholeness of the electron or photon cannot be made visible by experimental means. If there is anything that is truly objective to us (that is, anything that we do not in some sense determine as participants while observing it) it is thus invisible. Things have their wholeness in the worldfield, not in the realm in which we can observe this or that aspect of them.

Complementarity in Ancient China

One way of helping ourselves to see the emerging myth may be to see that it is indeed a motif that has been with us for three thousand years. The Chinese symbol for the connected oppositeness of things is the *t'ai chi t'u*, or "Diagram of the Great Ultimate," sometimes also rendered as "Diagram of the Primal Beginning." Its symbol is shown once again in Figure 3.1.

The dark and light parts of the diagram represent the two primal energies, yin and yang, respectively. The two drop-shaped forms intertwine and dance together, but in the heart of each is the other, as a small dot. That means that the two powers can never be separated; they are polar opposites, but united. This is a clear symbol of complementarity. The most ancient source of the philosophy of these primal energies is the *Book of Changes*, which is thought to have acquired most of its present form before 1100 B.C.E. This text holds the primary place among the sources of Chinese thought. It contains the Great Commentary, which opens as follows:

Figure 3:1: T'ai Chi T'u, the Diagram of the Great Ultimate

Heaven is high, the earth is low; thus the Creative and the Receptive are determined. . . . Movement and rest have their definite laws; according to these, firm and yielding lines are differentiated.[3]

The term "lines" refers to certain symbols discussed in the text. These symbols are called "hexagrams," for each consists of six lines. The first hexagram is "Heaven," or "the Creative," and consists of six *yang* lines, ——, and the second is "Earth," or "the Receptive," consisting of six *yin* lines, — —. (See Figure 3.2.)

Yang is also firm and bright, while yin is yielding and dark. These are the opposites of which everything is formed. In the philosophy of change, yang takes on energy and changes to yin, and vice versa. There are sixty-four possible combinations of yang and yin lines, thus sixty-four hexagrams in the book, which comprise all possible situations. Actually, there are many more specific situations, for any or all of the lines may be in the state of being about to change into the other kind. Which lines are about to change, if any, comes to light in the process of consulting the book for a description of any situation of interest. A yang line in this state is called an "old yang" line, and similarly, a yin line about to change is called "old yin." When the one quality dies, the other is born. These changes are also written in the Great Treatise, where it says:

Heaven, the Creative   *Earth, the Receptive*

Figure 3.2: First and Second Hexagrams from the Book of Changes

The [images] succeed one another by turns, as the firm and the yielding displace each other.[4]

The point here is the representation of complementarity in the duality of manifestation in the yang and the yin, and the changes from one to the other. This quite nicely reflects the ability of an electron to manifest itself as wave or as particle.

Heaven and earth are, of course, not so far from the ultimate opposites of spirit and matter. There is another profound link between this ancient system and its modern counterpart. As the One (the unchanging background, the field, called the *Tao*) begets the Two (yang and yin), the Two beget a Third, namely humanity. As the text tells us:

The movements of the six lines contain the ways of the three primal powers.[5]

That is, the upper two lines are the place of heaven, the lower two of earth, and the middle two of humanity, the third "primal power" in the Chinese system.

This situation corresponds quite precisely to our present understanding of psyche (humanity) as coming into being between spirit (heaven) and matter (earth), and compounded of both. In this regard, I want to repeat a brief quotation from Jung, already given in chapter 1:

Matter and spirit both appear in the realm of the psyche as distinctive qualities of conscious contents. The ultimate nature of both is transcendental, that is, irrepresentable, since the psyche and its contents are the only reality which is given to us without a medium.[6]

I do not believe it possible to overstress this triad of spirit and matter and the psyche arising from them.

Anaximander's Apeiron

Anaximander was a student of Thales and was his successor as a teacher. He lived from approximately 610 to 545 B.C.E. In the Greek world of the time, thinkers were trying to conceive of the origination of the world and of things. Some took one of the four elements, fire, air, water, or earth, as the source of the others. Anaximander thought that the source must be beyond any one of them and conceived of the *apeiron*, or the boundless, as that source. Many ancient writers have given their opinions as to what Anaximander meant by the *apeiron*, and some have concluded that he meant a state in which nothing was separate from anything else. That is, *apeiron* means a state without any boundaries within itself, rather than something that is infinite with regard to space.

This world-forming stuff was thus unlike anything that exists in the visible world, something indefinite. It was without beginning, ageless, and indestructible, and surrounded all things. It was beyond human imagination, since it held the opposites. Thales had thought that water was the prime substance, but Anaximander would have reasoned that since water is opposed by fire, and that they mutually destroy each other, one of the elements by itself could not give birth to the others. Fire and water are distinct, so their common source must be indefinite, that is, *apeiron*.

Apparently Aristotle identified the *apeiron* with the divine, as in the following quotation, although it is not quite clear whether Aristotle or Anaximander is making the identification:

And this is the divine, for it is immortal and indestructible, as Anaximander says and most of the physicists.[7]

As for Anaximander himself, for all the ancient description of his system, we have only one fragment of direct quotation, but it is about the origin and annihilation of the opposites. It is quoted by Aristotle's successor, Theophrastus:

Whence things arise, thence they also pass away; so it must be, for they violate and compensate each other in their disjunction, within the structure of time.[8]

That is to say, the opposites are continually at war with each other, encroaching on one another, balancing their effects, and at last they annihilate each other and return to the *apeiron*.

This description could also be used of the origin of the building blocks of our modern chemical elements, as they precipitated out of the primeval fireball of the Big Bang according to current theory.

Again, Aristotle, referring to Anaximander, says that the opposites are "separated out from the One, being present in it." This type of creation from the worldfield, in which two entities arise that are opposites, accords exactly with our modern notion of complementarity. And the fact that the opposites stay related to each other, even in hostility, to the point of mutual annihilation, similarly matches the complementarity discovered by science.

Of course, these are mythic motifs, and it has been the aim of science to demythologize reality. The fact is, however, that that aim cannot be accomplished, for our worldview is our myth of the moment. It might be better to say that ancient intuition hit on some deep realities, although at the time there would be no way to choose among speculative alternatives those images that would turn out to be the right ones at later times. That is why it is necessary also to give some scientific justification for saying that the emerging worldview reflects these ancient motifs.

Paradox is the very fiber of literature and poetry, not to mention theological discourse, and these same motifs have had rich lives through the ages. Although it would be impossible to attempt even a moderate sampling, the first few that come to mind will probably provide enough stimulation for further thought. The idea of the source that is also the goal is reflected in images such as that of Genesis 3:19: "For dust you are, and to dust you shall return," or the opening of Nikos Kazantzakis' *Saviors of God*: "We come from a dark abyss, we end in a dark abyss, and we call the luminous interval life."[9] The realm of luminosity, the visible realm, is visible precisely because it is the world of contrasts. Our very consciousness is paradoxical.

Separation and Inclusion

Complementarity helps us interpret many opposites that affect our lives, including heart/mind, individual/community, spirit/matter, and many others. Each of these pairs has a separating member and an inclusive member. In the wave/particle pair, the wave aspect (continuity) is inclusive, while the particle aspect (discontinuity) is separative. If the two members of the pair are to form a unitary whole, the inclusive member must include the separating member in spite of the separation. Opposites can make up a whole only if each of them subtly includes the other.

As we have seen in the Chinese "Diagram of the Great Ultimate," in Figure 3.1 above, the opposites are symbolized by the black and white portions. (We might assign the black to the inclusive side, for it provides the border that defines the whole.) Each major half contains a dot of the other color.

The rational/nonrational pair can be said to be the theme of this whole book. It also can be used to describe almost any of the other pairs of opposites. Thus, the rational, or separating member, finds the nonrational at its heart, and the same model holds for the inclusive element, which cannot be itself without the separating one, just as our psyches cannot truly be healed without our first acknowledging the reality of our wounds.

A theological example comes to mind, inspired by a sermon of Paul Tillich, in which the opposites are sin and grace.[10] The sermon is based on Paul's words in Romans 5:20: "Moreover the law entered, that the offense might abound. But where sin abounded, grace did much more abound." Sin is the separating member of the pair, and grace is the inclusive member. In the model of complementarity, then, grace must include sin in spite of the power of separation embodied in sin itself. For "sin" we could substitute alienations of all sorts, and for "grace" we could substitute all forms of acceptance and inclusiveness. Acceptance overcomes alienation, including the alienation that has occurred between religion and science as such.

Paradigm Shifts

Worldviews change slowly, whether in individuals or in whole societies. The current worldview will be particularly slow to change because it is easier to hold a one-sided outlook than to hold opposite outlooks simultaneously. I love ease as well as anyone and know well the pain of being confronted with my failure to risk in relationships and in work. I think of my own escapism as a manifestation of my participation in the rationalistic paradigm against which I argue in the scientific arena.

A paradigm shift is not a matter of intellectual understanding. It hits us where we *feel*. The mistaken idea that it is primarily an intellectual enterprise is part of the rationalistic worldview. What we are talking about is much deeper in the psyche. Because it is so deep, the words and facts that I offer here cannot by themselves convince someone who subscribes to the rationalistic worldview. As the proverb goes, "Those convinced against their will are of the same opinion still." To change our worldview, something must speak to our wholeness. When it does, our wholeness will respond with its assent and a move toward change. It will accept the newly revealed aspect of reality.

Argumentation and demonstration are merely the surface of the paradigm shift, though they must be presented. What is real to us lies in our depths, and though external facts do have an impact on our psychic structure, that structure changes only slowly. The deep nature of human paradigm shifts taking place over decades can be seen, for example, in the slowness and difficulties accompanying the change of the status of African-Americans and women in American society and in the military. Some shifts require centuries.

A new paradigm begins to arise when new facts contradict the unconscious assumptions contained in the old worldview. Clearly, the new paradigm cannot be understood, much less validated, from within the old. However, the facts that challenge the validity of the old view arise from within the activities of those practicing the existing myth. Thus, at least the need for a transformation can be demonstrated from within the worldview that is passing away.

For many of us—for all of us at one time or

another—the facts and their implications are obscured by the tenacity, in the psyche, of the old worldview itself. Questions are often raised as to the scientific validity of theories arising within the new science, such as complementarity. That is, the demand is that the new view be validated within the old. The whole notion of scientific validity is changing, however, and new grounds for validity must be discovered. Since physical reality itself is nonrational, the demands of rationalism cannot be met. Therefore, reductionism, as a final position unmodified by wholeness, is simply wrong, though as a method it has its uses.

The facts now require a new approach that denies the demands of rationalism. However, a new understanding is emerging to deal with the physical facts we have discovered, namely complementarity, a view that is nonrational, yet structured. It is now possible to see the nature of reality from within the next-level model. The new skin of the serpent is forming even as the old one is shed, to continue a metaphor from the previous chapter.

Rationalism, pursued to its extreme, runs into the nonrational, so that logical extremism becomes logical fallacy. Even mathematics ran up against this truth in the 1931 work by Kurt Gödel on "undecidable theorems." He proved that logical systems that are at least as complex as arithmetic cannot be demonstrated to be self-consistent, and that to be complete, a logical system must have an infinite number of axioms.[11] This is the same sort of situation as that which arose experimentally in physics, leading to complementarity. We might well say that these results are nonrational, and they were just as disturbing to mathematicians as complementarity has been to physicists.

Left-Brain Addiction

For those who have devoted their lives to "figuring things out," it is difficult to let the wholeness speak; for rational knowledge, which I will also refer to as "contrast-knowledge," separates us from the view of the wholeness of things. Those who use the left (rational) brain to its ultimate actually do us a great service, in that they bring about the discoveries that make our lives physically easier. However, they can also get trapped or addicted. Specialists tend to see things from an extremely limited perspective. A military specialist, for example, can easily become addicted to methods that depend upon military power; similarly, physicists can be dazzled by the power of mathematics and other forms of deductive reasoning to describe phenomena.

Rationalism denies the many nonrational ways of knowing, which include everything of which we say we "feel" that it is such-and-such a way. In *Personal Knowledge,* Michael Polanyi describes the way in which a scientist senses an immanent scientific discovery by "feeling" its proximity.[12] Other examples include the interpretation of facial expressions, and all forms of nonverbal communications. The skilled use of our bodies is a feeling thing in the same sense. A basketball player, for instance, often can "feel" that the ball will go into the net at the instant the shot is made. This, too, is nonrational. Other examples include all noncausal meaningful coincidences of inner (psychic) and outer (physical) states, already discussed as synchronicity. The whole realm of meaning as applied to living is nonrational.

Those who speak for the paradigm shift from reductionism to complementarity are viewed by many within standard physics as doing a disservice to science. Perhaps we might draw an apt metaphor from the study of addiction. When family members intervene in the lives of alcoholics and try to make them enter treatment, the alcoholics often consider that act to be a disservice, because they are in denial about their addiction. This is what seems to be happening in standard science. It seems that the left brain—generally viewed as analytic, rational, and separative—is not capable of hospitalizing itself; it cannot see what it is leaving out of the total picture, or it simply has no interest in the wholeness of reality. It is the *intervention of the wholeness aspect of the person* that enables ego-consciousness to see its sickness. When it does, it is already on the way to healing. The solution to the problem of living as seen by an alcoholic is more alcohol. It appears to be the same with left-brain addiction. A scientist within the current paradigm will say that standard science can solve the problems of contradictory facts, whatever they may be, an approach that completely neglects other means of knowing, and assumes that only an answer in the rationalistic mode will suffice.

Electrons in Atoms

In order to bring about a healing of our worldview, we must examine the current view and learn to see through it. And, to do that, we must look at that view somewhat from within it. One means of bringing out the contradictions in that view is to consider what electrons are when they are in atoms. This is also the area in which many physicists still have difficulty accepting the reality of the wave state. We need to see why the electron in an atom cannot be a particle.

A photograph of a model of a particular electron pattern in a hydrogen atom is shown in Figure 3.3a. A hydrogen atom consists of a proton, which carries most of the massiveness of the atom, and an electron, which is

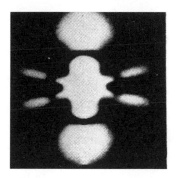

Figure 3.3a: Modern Model of Electron Pattern in Hydrogen Atom. Source: Harvey E. White, Pictorial representations of the electron cloud for hydrogen-like atoms. Physical Review 37, 1416–1434.

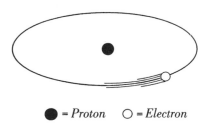

● = *Proton*   **○** = *Electron*

Figure 3.3b: Traditional Depiction of Electron in Hydrogen Atom.

traditionally seen as whirling around the proton in an orbit (Figure 3.3b).

The mutual electrical attraction of the proton and the electron keeps the electron from flying off, just as the moon is held in its orbit around the earth by the mutual gravitation of the two bodies. This view of the atom, first proposed by Niels Bohr in 1913, still depicts the proton and electron as particles.

In Figure 3.3a the whole fuzzy image is that of a single electron. This image is certainly very different from Figure 3.3b, and so it should be; in an atom, the electron is in its wave state. But we need to fill in some of the details of how we know this.

By 1915 even the most reluctant physicists had concluded that the particle nature of electromagnetic energy (including light) was undeniable; the wave and particle natures of photons were equally real. Previously it had been thought that light came only in wave form, and experiments had convincingly confirmed its wave nature. Einstein's explanation, published in 1905, of the experimental results that demonstrated the particle nature of light were so shocking that it took ten years for physicists to convince themselves that he was correct.

In the early 1920s, the corresponding wave nature of electrons (previously thought of only as particles) was demonstrated, but in spite of this proof many physicists, even Nobel laureates, have been unable to release themselves from the particle view of electrons that are "bound" in atoms.

In 1925, a rule known as Heisenberg's Uncertainty Principle was added to the foundations of quantum theory, the new physics of subatomic entities. While wave and particle are *qualitative* aspects of microphysical entities, the uncertainty principle applies to the measurement of certain *quantities* that can be measured with respect to an electron, such as position, time, energy, and momentum.

Just as the wave and particle aspects of elementary entities exclude each other (that is, are contradictory), these other physical quantities show a similar kind of exclusion, in that refining the knowledge of one of them blurs the knowledge of another. One such pair of quantities, which interact with each other so that the precision of one excludes the precision of the other, is the pair energy/time: the energy contained in a given physical configuration can be precisely known only if that energy remains stable long enough so that the time interval involved is very wide (blurry). If we want to narrow down the time interval, the amount of energy involved becomes blurred. The other major pair of quantities governed by the uncertainty principle are position (location) and momentum.

While the uncertainty principle is usually presented in terms of attempts to measure the quantities involved, and

I presented them so myself in introducing them, that presentation is actually misleading. The principle holds whether actual measurements are taken or not. Any physical conditions that "confine" the value of one of the physical quantities in question have repercussions on the other quantity in the pair. The uncertainty principle seems to be about the quantities themselves, not about their measurement, unless we say that the universe *measures itself* by actualizing various forms, from atoms to stars (in which case we open things up to profundities of a different sort). The important point here is that the operation of the uncertainty principle does not depend at all upon the presence or intervention of our ego-consciousness in the situation in an attempt to know or measure something.

Perhaps the prime example is the fact that until the advent of the uncertainty principle, physicists thought of the atomic nucleus as consisting of protons and electrons, rather than protons and neutrons, as they do today. The uncertainty principle showed that if an electron were confined in such a small volume as the nucleus (in other words, if its position became precise) it would possess so much momentum, or speed, that it would simply burst out (its momentum would become large and "blurred"). No measurements were invoked here— only the precondition that the electron be confined to the nucleus. The uncertainty principle then tells us what the consequence of that precondition will be.

Bohr and Heisenberg together concluded that the uncertainty principle was a consequence of the complementarity of particles and waves.[13] In fact, the uncertainty principle excludes the particle nature for electrons that are components of, or "bound to," atoms, because by being in the atom, an electron's location is so precise or confined that its momentum is too large or "blurred" for it to be in an orbit. Only "free" (un-bound) electrons can be in the particle state.

The Reality of the Wave State

Some physicists still insist that the uncertainty principle only says that we cannot know the orbit, but that wave forms (see Fig. 3a, above) still represent the probability of finding "the electron" in a given place. That is, they still conceive of the electron as a hard tiny particle actually moving along a path somewhere among a virtual cloud of such possible pathways, which they call a "probability cloud." That is why I have stressed the fact that the uncertainty principle is not really about measurement, but about the state or condition of the electron itself. Our knowing or not knowing which state the electron is in is irrelevant.

Even more significantly, if the electron in an atom were a particle that were moving round and round a nucleus (even if we could not assign it a path), it would become a little energy transmitter and radiate away the energy that kept it in orbit. This is the argument about the collapse of matter mentioned in chapter 2. However, because the electron is a wave in the atom, it is not subject to this law of radiation.

An electron bound to an atom is in its "wave" state, which is sometimes called the "quantum state." Its wave properties give a complete picture of its existence when in an atom. Thus it makes no sense to envision an electron in an atom as a particle in a probability cloud. The *reality* of the wave state—the fact that the wave truly is the *electron itself*—holds the greatest scientific explanatory power.

Although it is indeed true that the physicists' picture of the probability cloud *also* gives the probability of "finding" the electron at any given point in the pattern, that picture is conceptually misleading, for to "find" (capture) the electron, we must destroy the wholeness of the atom. In that case, the question simply remains unanswered as to what the electron *is* when it is in the atom undisturbed.

Only a creative transformation of science to something more whole (more true to the whole of reality) will enable it to support the nonrational dimension; standard science cannot do so. Accepting the experimental studies that have shown that photons and electrons can exhibit logically contradictory qualities will be a major step in this transformation. What I have given here is simply the best interpretation of the experiments within the framework of present human ego-consciousness, which can only perceive things in terms of such contrasts as wave and particle. In time, complementarity will become a new standard for physics, awaiting its own overturning from some unexpected quarter.

The Intervention of Wholeness

Wholeness, or the field, expresses itself through the facts that it places in our path, to see or not to see, as seeing becomes possible through our growth. If we are one-sided in some respect, the corrective is generally there in some form, knocking on the door.

Standard physics, as the true offspring of our separating consciousness, the perception of that which is merely our ego, can only focus on the matter aspect of reality, and necessarily neglects the spirit, for the latter cannot be quantified and measured. The myth of physics is the spiritlessness of nature, which Teilhard de Chardin sought to correct by coining the term "spirit-matter." A spirit-matter cosmos is a different myth, certainly, but one that supports more facts.

The wholeness of the stuff of which our universe is made includes both.

The worldview that seems to be emerging will be no more final than those of the past have been. There are, and always will be, other ways of conceiving atoms than the way creatures do so at any given time. Some of them might be imaginable to us at present if we were more open, but some are necessarily beyond any imagination we now possess. When we come upon them, we will do so on the basis of fact. Yet when we do come to them, we cannot accept them as the ultimate revelation. We are never free of illusion, however penetrating our gaze. We cannot discern things as they are in themselves. This is the reason why there never will be a final theory, a "theory of everything," as some refer to it, but only theories that come closer to deep reality—a more and more effective myth of being.

The parallels of science and religion are quite striking here. At our best, we know that we can make no final statement concerning God, though we can attest to a whole range of human experience that leads us to speak of God. It is only curious how different the god-concepts that arise out of numinous experience are with respect to each other. We go wrong mainly in thinking that *our* concept of God describes the "true God," and that others are less valid. The same is true in science, and the influences of cultural worldviews on conceptions of matter and the cosmos are not difficult to document. When the Japanese physicist Yukawa was asked how it was possible that he had conceived of "mesons" as particles that hold an atomic nucleus together, when so many great Western physicists had not thought of the correct solution, he replied: "You see, we in the East have not been corrupted by Aristotle."[14]

In the West, rationalism has been falsely used to

anchor our being. We hang on to it as if it were the living support of our existence, intellectual or otherwise. To the above description of the nonrationality of the electron we say, "Yes, but how am I to *understand* that?" This question assumes that the only answer that will satisfy us or give us security is the rational one. But even when language is as clean and consistent as possible, it still can never make nonrational things rational, and this is the point: phenomena are nonrational, and *all rationalism fails to provide an anchor for living.* Logicians say, "But if an assertion and its opposite (e.g., an electron is a wave, and an electron is a particle) are both true, then all assertions are true." In logic this is indeed the case, but if the world did have such a rational ground, it would be a disaster, for electrons would only be particles, and atoms would collapse. Electrons must be waves in atoms, as noted earlier. The very stability of matter thus depends on the nonrational ability of electrons to be waves as well as particles, as needed.

The physical world is not obliged to uphold our assumption of rationalism. It is simultaneously true, first, that real physical entities manifest qualities that are logically contradictory, and second, that the world is not a chaotic profusion in which every imaginable thing is true. Real things exhibit some properties and not others. Logic is not the ground of being!

The old myth has been that of objectivity and rationalism. To say that these ideals were a myth is only to say that they constituted the prevailing view of the universe. Now we are shifting to a new one, the new myth. Because we can never know things as they are in themselves, we must always hold to the best symbolic expression of the way things are that we can find. Science at its "hardest" can still only be symbolic, that is, mythic. It gives us a way of describing reality that is often very effective. Yet we can now be confident that things are quite other than science has described them. And they are quite other than they are described in the worldview of complementarity, though that view can be expected to increase the effectiveness of science for some time to come, and to restore much of what it was for in the first place, namely to help us to discover who and what we are.

CHAPTER FOUR

The Divergence of Science and Religion

As it reveals itself in beings, Being withdraws.
—*Martin Heidegger,* Early Greek Thinking

The convergence of science and religion must be seen as a reconnection of the two, since they originally arose together in the human psyche. That is, to understand the need for the convergence of science and religion we must first understand their gradual divergence, from ancient times to the present. Science and religion are complementary ways of knowing. That is, they arose as opposites from within an original whole. (See the model for the emergence of such opposites at the beginning of chapter 1.) In the story of their splitting apart and reconvergence, we have yet another example of complementarity.

It was not at first apparent how distinct these two ways of viewing the world were, or how distinct the questions were that motivate each. Singly or together, science and religion constitute a search for the *ground of being,* that is, the basis for our existence, and for clues, if any, to why things happen as they do. As experience accumulates, the questions that drive these fields of inquiry become more refined and head in increasingly divergent directions. Seeing the parts leads us in the direction of matter, and seeing the wholes leads in the direction of spirit. In earlier times, however, each study was felt to be seeking knowledge of nature as a whole, for nature was not only fascinating to the reasoning mind but alive with spirit, with the divine.

We now seek to restore a balance in the relationship between seeing the whole and seeing the parts of creation. To see only the whole or only the parts is false to the nature of reality. The blindness of science to the wholeness of life has led many to view it as exclusively destructive, but religion has its destructive side as well, epitomized in "holy wars" around the world through the ages. Both science and religion hold many benefits for humanity. It is our responsibility to urge them to their creative ends.

The Rise of Rationalism

Humans are avid diggers at the roots of things; we want to get back to origins. We assume that when we have done so we will understand who we are and why we are here. This digging is also what we might call "the quest of the One," and so it is paradoxical: we hope for simplicity, but what we find is more and more complex, especially when pursued with all our rational powers.

The rational approach to problems and to understanding is to divide a problem or a situation to be understood into small elements that can be dealt with more simply. This approach is a powerful tool for acquiring not only understanding, but freedom as well. With this method in mind, I will define rationalism as the assumption that this divisive process can be carried through to the point that one does, in fact, reach that which is ultimately simple, clear, and distinct. We might call this the "particle theory" of concepts and knowledge.

The ancient Greeks sought to discover, by reasoning from the visible nature of things, a "first element" or "first principle" from which all else follows. And many philosophers have concerned themselves with the search for the simplest categories of which thought is composed, which are conceived to be necessarily exactly what they are and which cannot be reduced to simpler elements.

By now we have encountered enough of complementarity to see that by insisting on the particle nature of knowledge rationalism neglects the seeing of wholes, and therefore aborts *meaning*. Rational science does not possess an internal guide as to its own limitations. To see its limitations, we must balance its rational approach with a holistic one, and recognize, as pointed out in the previous chapter, that logical extremism is a major logical fallacy. But how are we to tell when we have reached the point at which rationalism is yielding diminishing returns? We cannot determine this point by rational means. We must also take into account the wholeness of things. And, in the words of Edward Teller quoted in the previous chapter, "It is necessary to adjust the two approaches in a manner that is by no means obvious."[1]

Science arises in our attempt to understand, to simplify, and to help ourselves by becoming less at the mercy of the ravages of nature, not to mention the wrath of divine powers. Let us consider again Thales' eclipse, the total solar eclipse of the year 585 B.C.E., which is the first known to have been predicted (chapter 2). Eclipses were widely thought to be free acts of gods to make their presence and will felt by humans. How different life becomes once eclipses are believed to be natural phenomena that can be predicted! On the one hand, scientific knowledge frees us from at least some anxiety as to whether an event is a message of divine wrath: we need not fear the eclipse. On the other hand, every advance of scientific knowledge seemingly forces the divine to recede into the distance, though this is not perceived by everyone at once. Even today disasters and outbreaks of disease are perceived by a number of people as evidence of divine displeasure. AIDS is a case in point.

In science, every differentiation or distinction that can be made becomes the basis for a division of categories. If specimen A has some differences from specimen B, we can describe the difference and open a new classification. Spiders and insects both have legs, but spiders have eight, while insects have six. Until we made that distinction, they were all just "bugs." This process is at the root of science. The role of counting and measurement in seeing differences is crucial to the rise of science as such, though the fundamental idea of seeing differences is the same. Measurement enables us to see finer and finer differences. For instance, by measuring repeatedly and carefully, we can deal with the proportions of parts in a jaw or a skull in a given animal form over time. Measurement also adds greatly to our sense of the *stability* of things in nature because many inanimate objects retain the same measurements for long periods.

It is said that the progress of science comes in obtaining "the next decimal place" in the accuracy of our measurements, because then we notice differences that would have gone unseen in well-known quantities, and that leads to changes in our whole worldview, as we saw in the case of Kepler (chapter 3).

We can now measure minute differences in the way that time passes for differently moving vehicles, as was predicted by Einstein's relativity. In other words, there is not one uniformly passing time for everyone, but each individual possesses a unique time. The fact that we can catch a bus or a plane and get to scheduled meetings is only possible because we all are moving relatively slowly, and the differences in our personal times is too small to detect, but we know it is there. It is actually possible to measure differences in time recorded on two atomic clocks when one is left in a stationary position and another is carried around the world on scheduled airline flights. Such fascinating discoveries owe their existence not only to the measurability of the physical world, but to our innate human curiosity about such things.

Even our cheapest wristwatches measure time accurately to within a few seconds a month, as compared to a few minutes a day fifty years ago. We are fascinated by such achievements, not least by their applications in computers and satellite communications. Anyone can now buy a pocket-sized locator that will give one's position on the earth to within a few meters; the device works by tuning in to a system of navigational satellites. To say that we have gained much benefit from the scientific way of approaching things is a tremendous understatement. It has given us the ability to adapt to virtually all of Earth's environments, and produced labor-saving devices that few of us would be willing to cast out.

Observing and classifying differences, breaking the world into smaller and smaller parts, has enabled us to understand causes; but it has also created its own problems—points of friction where the interpretations of rationalistic science run counter to the facts concerning the wholeness of existence and life—or we would not now be seeking a reunion of science and religion.

The Eclipse of the Divine

At one time, the adventure of understanding was a single enterprise, with the divine felt as permeating the world. It is difficult for us to recreate for ourselves the feelings of earlier times, of being so much more fully at the mercy of unknown powers. We may perhaps imagine the discovery of agriculture: the fear and daring of penetrating Mother Earth; the sense of power and hope, in directing work toward a future, not fully assured, harvest; the feeling of dependence upon divine powers to provide for the conditions of growing; the knowledge that in the seed lies the power of rebirth. Here is a full and fertile mix of science and religion. In the same vein, we may re-image the ancient Egyptian priests guarding the knowledge of the timing of flooding of the Nile, which brought a new layer of fertile soil to the land yearly, when the star Sirius was seen to rise just before the sun. Did the priests see this knowledge as essentially religious or were they holding science hostage to religion for the sake of political power? I lean toward the former view, but either way we see clearly the interweaving of science and spirit, and the sacred nature of knowledge with its reward of divine benefits. In his book *Myth and Symbol in Ancient Egypt*, R.T.R. Clark says:

Egyptian religion . . . penetrated and informed every aspect of life. The Greeks were the first to discover spheres of activity which were independent of religion or to be expressed in non-religious terms. Since then—but only intermittently—the West has been accustomed to set experience into two divisions, Church and State, religion and science. The Egyptians belonged to the pre-Greek era; for them there was no dichotomy.[2]

In Egypt, the bringing of knowledge to humans, including music, writing, agriculture, and measurement, was attributed to gods, the culture bringers, the first saviors. In ancient Egypt this role belonged to the god Osiris, first as the promiser of agricultural renewal, but later as the giver of all the arts of civilization. In some theological systems, these were attributed to Thoth. The bringing of civilization was also the bringing of order, and that certainly included measurement and mathematics. Science and civilization are close kin, and they are divine gifts in any case.

Only after millennia of an ordered agricultural life might the bold and heretical thought arise that laws of Nature simply *existed*, without the help of gods. This transition might be like that which we experience as children when, in a moment of crisis, we learned that "cross my heart and hope to die" can be spoken with impunity. The first time that sentence is spoken, with maybe some fudging of the truth, we wonder whether we have indeed sentenced ourselves to eternal death; but at some point we gradually learn that the world is not that simple. What a blend of joy and sorrow, fear and power, fills us then, at that fatal and lifegiving transformation of the world and of personal being. This personal experience, as part of growing up, is the essential counterpart of the divergence of science and religion in cultural history. We learn that, scientifically speaking, we do not die, but we also learn to forget that something of wholeness in us does indeed die if we make a habit of untruth. Whether or not the child becomes cynical depends on what values have been established in him or her up to that moment. Of course, these values can either be religious (focusing on divine powers) or humanistic (focusing on inherent human capacities).

With the emergence of a much more secular world and the idea of democracy, with its more generalized education, learning began to be subtly distinguished from living. Socrates, who castigated the Sophists for commercializing learning, was tried for threatening the established religion because he took his intense questioning style to the streets, attracting youth to self-examination and doubt, and perhaps encouraging them to be less subservient to external authority.

While the divergence of science and religion began in the Greek invention of the secular world, it bore fruit much later. It took centuries for the critical intellect to evolve a fully rationalistic outlook. It also took a long time for the psyche to feel free to turn the annihilating gaze of its rationalism directly upon cultural archetypes, the inwardly held views of the "way things are," which are bound up in religions.

Both science and religion pride themselves on their separate devotions to the habit of truth. For that reason, both of them are forms of human innocence, as opposed to the cynicism characteristic of those devoted to political and economic power for its own sake, the disciples of Machiavelli, as it were. But we are following the divergence that occurred in the stream of human sincerity, and must let the study of human cynicism go.

From ancient Greece to the time of Descartes, higher learning essentially remained unified in its concern for both values and knowledge. The psychological integrity of the whole was not severely threatened for two thousand years. Reason was considered a divine gift, and philosophers did indeed pray for divine help with their thoughts. Values were a topic of keen interest, and the learning process proceeded within an overarching cultural-religious milieu.

One of these cultural values was the idea of kingship and royalty, especially where divine right to rule had been accepted for long periods. In sixteenth-century Europe it was effectively the case that whatever religion was held by the ruler would be the religion of the people of that land. While the connection between royalty and religion is not necessarily rooted in the sacred scripture of any given religion, the idea of a king is fundamentally religious. The institution of kingship in Israel is a very explicit case. According to that story, when the people feared that God could not provide sufficient guidance and security, they asked the prophet Samuel to have God send a king to govern them. As described in 1 Samuel 8:7, their lack of confidence aroused God's anger and scornful observation: "They have rejected me from being king over them." Later, the prophet Micah chided the people with this memory: "Why do you cry out; is there no king in you?" (Micah 4.9).

In the Middle Ages, philosophy and theology were still intimate, even during the struggle of reason for a position of power in the relationship of the two. The spiritual impulse tends to restrain reason. Philosophers took to heart the words of Zechariah 2:17: "Be silent, all flesh, before the Lord." They believed that the uses of reason were to be limited to the understanding of God and revelation. We must remember that this struggle went on in individual humans who *felt* the conflict between science and religion internally. Religious individuals such as Abelard, Albertus Magnus, and Roger Bacon took risks on behalf of the intrinsic value of reason and the understanding of nature to provide a place for reason and revelation alike in their lives. Theirs was an engagement or struggle within a yet unbroken whole, which was nonetheless destined to push the worlds of science and religion asunder.

Reason became identified with science, and the restraint of reason on the part of faith with religion. It was not until much later that reasoning in spiritual matters really came into its own (see chapter 6). Where the power of a primordial faith—a previously unbroken faith, as distinct from a broken and reestablished faith—is sufficiently strong, reason can be tolerated. The Church could at least permit mystical reasoning, as opposed to naturalistic reasoning. History does not show us a continuous rise of reason as a power against faith, but rather a seesaw movement. In the end, it will show us a loosening of more primitive kinds of faith, to be displaced by more mature varieties. Faith does not lose the contest, because of the non-rational nature of the universe, which reason ultimately cannot conquer. The ultimate mystery is safe by its own nature.

As we have seen, it is a general mythic and psychological pattern that an unbroken whole gives rise to conflicting offspring. From the warring brothers Horus and Set in Egyptian mythology, to the evolution of left- and right-brain functional differences, the pattern is abundantly amplified. The pattern fits the photon and electron also, where each gives rise to conflicting wave and particle phenomena. The same applies to our picture of childhood as such a whole, and of maturity as the capacity to handle the tension of opposites. With regard to the relationship of science and religion, we might say that humanity is now in an adolescent stage of growth: the whole is broken, and society feels deeply the tensions of the conflict of such seeming opposites. We need growth and maturity to bind up the fragments.

"Enlightenment"

Another major movement in the divergence of science and religion took place in the West from the sixteenth through the eighteenth centuries and includes the emigrations from Europe to the Americas. Our system of higher education in the United States owes its very existence to the Protestant Reformation, with its proclamation of the priesthood of all believers. To fulfill this vision, the people had to be educated in order to understand the scriptures. An educated clergy was held to be the foundation of the new nation. This gives a marvelous example of an unbroken cultural-religious archetype, for it was not generally feared that education would endanger the health of religion. That is, religious belief seemed securely in place as a norm in human affairs. When Harvard College was founded, the Enlightenment was still a century in the future, and during that century many other colleges were begun in what would become the United States.

The Enlightenment brought forth modern rationalism, with its slow but steady erosion of primordial religion. Some of its proponents, such as Thomas Jefferson, saw religion as harmful to humans, and science as the path of salvation. Others embraced Enlightenment values and held them alongside their conventional religious views. Matters continued in this indecisive manner until that archetypal event of twentieth-century America, the Scopes trial, which pitted science and religion as direct antagonists, as both were understood at the time. The "trial" of evolution brought the conflict between these belief systems to the attention of a wide public, and thus was a major force in the evolution of the culture as a whole.

This trial was an important event. Though there were protagonists of a pure humanism during the whole span from at least Lucretius (around 60 B.C.E.) onward, the influence of their ideas was slow in developing. Even the writers of the Enlightenment, so negative in their assessments of religion, held to deeply ingrained and unconscious notions of morality, ethics, and human rights and purposes—notions that they drew from Christianity, but redesignated as "inalienable human" things. In the Declaration of Independence, Jefferson (and the other members of the congress) acknowledged a "creator's" role, though the expressed right to "life, liberty, and the pursuit of happiness" is distinctly secular in orientation.

In a sense, the Scopes trial was a reawakening of the age-old contest for supremacy between reason and scriptural revelation, or between scientific knowledge and belief. A new element in the contest as it now emerged was the fact that

Christianity was a religion that claimed the *historical* appearance of God. It thus inserted itself directly into the province of scientific exploration. Prior to such an assertion science and religion each, to a point, could simply go their own ways.

The asserted supremacy of reason (and the insistence upon natural causes for things) is the thrust of both science and philosophy, as against religion's stress upon revelation and belief. The separation of the two is made possible by a gradual loss of numinous experience, by what we call becoming jaded, or by mistaking a certain intensity of thrill for true numinosity or awe. Science and reason hold a certain kind of power that is indeed thrilling, but the sense that "this is rationally explained" tends to cut us off from seeing the true infinity within every physical happening. The explanation is always more partial than it appears.

Becoming entangled in the details of "all that there is to know," we lose sight of how much of our lives actually flows in a nonrational manner. This is a very regrettable loss; for the withering of numinous experience is something to be mourned. But we also need to include our rational faculties in living. We need to find that to which we can hold with integrity, which may well take us some distance from the religion of our upbringing. At the same time, we must continually renew the sources of numinous experience. Our intellectual integrity must be broadened to include the integrity of the whole.

Modern Times

The period since the Renaissance has witnessed the birth of modern science. Descartes' version of mind-body dualism is really the completion of the separation of earth and sky, matter and spirit. With Descartes, modern rationalism was fully launched, but it still took centuries for "science" to separate itself more completely from philosophy. Even until the late nineteenth century, science was considered a compartment of philosophy called "natural philosophy." As late as Newton's time, some almost animistic conceptions lingered in the terminology of physics. What we now call energy, for example, was called *vis viva,* or "living force." In his *Principia,* Newton asserted that the fact of action-at-a-distance (as in the case of gravity, for instance) proved the necessity of God, for in his time rational causality was only comfortable with forces involving the contact of bodies.[3] This preference is also related to trust of the senses, especially that of sight: "Seeing is believing."

Although Newton's *Principia* ends with God, from the point of view of modern science, this only shows the tenacity of the human feeling for spirituality. By the twentieth century, the greatest scientists still debated informally with each other as to the meaning of the "central order" of things. Yet on principle they excluded God from their professional work.

The philosophical principle closest to the attitude of modern (rationalistic) science is "Occam's Razor": Good theory minimizes assumptions; the simplest explanation that can account for the phenomena is most likely the true one. When Pierre Laplace presented his *System of the World* to the emperor Napoleon, he was asked why God was not mentioned in his book. He is said to have replied that he had no need of that hypothesis. Needless to say, Occam's Razor is effective in cutting off the spirit from science: God can never be a component of a scientific explanation. The modern attitude is that physics requires physical explanation. Although just what "physical" means remains cloudy, it certainly does not include God.

Besides Occam's Razor, philosophy presents us with the general attitude of skepticism, which has an even longer history. If I tell you something and you doubt it, that forces me to go deeper with my explanation. According to the principles of rationalistic scholarship, we should all doubt everything we hear, until we are given sufficient proof that the explanation given is the only one possible. However, the fact that not even the most hardened rationalist can actually live under this intellectual regime should help us to pause and question the completeness of the rationalistic approach as a way of life. While it is clear that God as an explanation for phenomena is always subject to doubt, we should also note well that ideas that have found universal acceptance within science (which seemed beyond doubt) have later given way to entirely new ways of looking at things, and will most likely continue to do so again and again. The prime example is that of Newton's idea of gravity giving way to Einstein's.

In short, to doubt what one cannot see and touch and to insist upon rational causal explanation via a minimum number of principles are sufficient to accomplish the separation of science from religion.

I am not recommending the abandonment of the tools of science that I have just described. The convergence of which I am speaking comes about through an entirely different means and does not require a relaxation of critical thinking, but the inclusion of a deeper acquaintance and understanding of the facts. In the end, only facts encountered within the methods of science can convince scientists of the nonrational nature of the universe.

Until then, the methods of science will exclude the things of the spirit. If these methods are given the status of final authority, the very real facts of the spirit will inevitably be discounted. The methods of science are, however, appropriate to some aspects of the human endeavor. This is as it should be, because the methods are not identical for all those who use them. One is free to use them while remaining aware of their limits. That is, whoever uses the classical methods of science should also be aware of the wholeness of things and the limitations of the reductive method.

These limitations come into play in that aspect of any question where the wholeness of a situation begins to play an essential part. If, for example, you devise an experiment to determine whether an electron is a particle or a wave, the experiment will give you a seemingly unequivocal answer. But another experiment can be devised that will give an answer that contradicts the answer given by the first experiment, and will do so with equal firmness, because at the subatomic level at which these experiments must be performed, we are bumping up against the wholeness of the electron, and rationalism there exceeds its limits. In the words of Kenneth Patchen (quoted in the epigraph to chapter 3 above): "Evidence conclusive, either way."[4]

Yet we cannot tell investigators to back off in any given case or forbid the methods of science. We would either fail to stop them in their pursuit of the facts, or we would fail to gain the insight that their pursuit might still have yielded. The methods of standard science promote contrast-knowledge and thereby also promote human freedom, including the freedom to cut ourselves off from the living depths of reality.

We see, though, that the spirit yet claims the human, and humans do attempt to bring the poles of life to a single wholeness. As we gradually replace the primordial bond with more mature spiritual aspirations, we will see that, as I said above, the secrets of the universe are ultimately safe, and that we may practice our reason as fully as we can imagine. Our only danger is to ourselves if we forget that reason is ultimately only one of two poles, the other of which is the nonrational wholeness of things. Because of this, there can be no limits even imagined for the progress of knowledge and understanding, nor for the spiritual growth of humanity and its inevitable successors in evolution.

While the inwardly felt force of the claim of the spirit, which we do indeed observe to move many of us, may be quite sufficient to carry the convergence forward, there is an even more compelling motivation to merge science and religion, as we find them now, into a single human enterprise. That is the fact that specific phenomena that fall within the purview of science now clearly defy the rationalism of the scientific method, and so redefine its role. That is, from this point forward, the practice of science must include the development of the spirit.

CHAPTER FIVE

The Mythic Roots of Consciousness

The development of consciousness in archetypal stages is a transpersonal fact, a dynamic self-revelation of the psychic structure which dominates human history.
Erich Neumann, The Origin and History of Consciousness

Freedom and consciousness emerge hand in hand. In the darkness of our animal past, there was no self-reflexivity as a basis for the awareness of options and values and for the power of choice. Wherever we are unconscious, wherever we cannot distance ourselves and reflect, we cannot be free. Contrast-based consciousness gives us a *vis-à-vis* relationship to both outer and inner reality and gives us images and language with which to relate creatively to both. On the other hand, as our rational awareness based on contrasts grows, our primordial awareness of the worldfield gradually diminishes. In religious language, we become cut off from God and are expelled from the Garden of Eden. The journey of humanity is to rediscover the place of our origin and know it for the first time, as Eliot said.

The model given in chapter 1 of the emergence of opposites from the worldfield is reflected in many ways in the story of the emergence of consciousness. In one sense, humanity has known of the model or motif of the separation of opposites from its beginnings, through its myths. The emergence of opposites is symbolized by the myth of the separation of the world-parents, which is found in virtually every culture. In the opening of the book of Genesis there are two divine acts of separation: light is created in the midst of darkness and the two are separated to make day and night; and waters are separated to make an expanse that is the sky. The Genesis story is a later and more abstract myth than most, but the same motif is present. Light and dark respectively symbolize consciousness and the unconscious that remains to surround the small region dimly illuminated with our awareness. The region above and below the region symbolize, among other things, spirit and matter. In the Babylonian separation myth, the waters, Apsu and Tiamat, are personified beings and more clearly the world-parents.

When opposites emerge, one of them has a separating nature, while the other is inclusive (see chapter 3). The emergence of consciousness from the unconscious follows the same model. In this case, our ego-consciousness is the separating element. It separates from (leaves behind, as it were) the whole of the unconscious field, except that now there is a layer in between, namely the specific unconscious that is the mate and immediate surroundings of this particular ego-consciousness.

Through our unconscious, we remain in contact with the field. That is, through the regulating function of the center of our individual being, which Jung termed the "Self," all that belongs to our life can come into contact with it. The well-known experience of meeting the right person at the right time is one example of this operation, as are the other instances of synchronicity discussed in chapter 1.

The Numinous

Our ordinary ego-consciousness is not the same as the deeper consciousness that we can achieve by a transformation of our attitude. Ego-consciousness is our everyday waking awareness that sees things by means of contrasts and learns by means of concepts. Our minds can easily assimilate knowledge in the rational mode, but what really counts is not what we know, but how we live. Learning to live in accord with the depths generally requires a moral integrative act, often amounting to nothing less than a far-reaching transformation of the personality. Seldom, if ever, does this occur without pain and suffering. Such a transformation is something that we undertake consciously, for the sake of deeper life itself.

Thus the deeper possibilities of consciousness require that we seek and align ourselves with what has been called the divine. We must find our depths and become more whole as humans. These depths are characterized, in part, by numinosity, the power of the divine within.

As long as we remain unconscious of the possibilities of deeper consciousness, our egos can masquerade as all there is to us; we can feel separate and self-sufficient. Until the discovery, over the last century, of the richness of the unconscious, we could claim that we are just what we think we are. Fortunately, that blind bliss is coming to an end.

The fact that the ascendancy of science and philosophy in the seventeenth century was called the Enlightenment is very symbolic of the thrill of power that attaches to achievements of the mind that are attained in a strictly intellectual way. That is one kind of power. But light need not be associated with the intellect alone. True, we have attained a brilliant sort of searchlight awareness that can turn this way and that, and can gather to itself the power of seeing more and more penetratingly into narrower and narrower regions. Light, however, can also be a gentle, holy glow or aura, so subtle that it may easily be missed in the blinding glare of our ego-consciousness.

The following words came to one of my teachers in a dream:

In the beginning, in the small and the great darkness, life is not Something; it ardently Is. Beginnings are not precision; beginnings are not confusion. They are darkness drawn to a minute point of nondarkness, and silence gathered into a small sound.[1]

Light that comes in this manner is *numen lumen*, holy light.

In *The Idea of the Holy*, Rudolf Otto made use of the terms *numinous* and *numinosity*, from *numen*, a Latin word for "holy power." For Otto, sensing the numinous involves having two main experiences, of a sort that cannot be easily be understood until one has had them. The first of these he calls "creature-feeling," where the word "feeling" means the perceived sense-perception that one is a "creature" (from the Latin word *creatura*, which means a created being), dependent upon something beyond oneself. It is easy for most of us to deaden ourselves to this kind of perception, the awareness of createdness, but it is a perception that is constantly available to us and often can be touched in meditation. Feeling insignificant in the vastness of the universe can also be a door to this experience if we somehow can retain the feeling that we carry purpose or meaning as well.

Otto then points to what he calls *mysterium tremendum*, which brings together the opposite notions of a quiet, mysterious encounter with the divine and the tremendous one that shakes us with its power, before which we tremble, even shudder. Without the element of mystery, however, an experience of power is only an empty thrill. Precisely because of the absence of mystery in our lives, we tend to seek ever greater shocks and thrills. This explains the fascination of our culture with "action movies." Some of the most grisly crimes are committed by persons who have lost the ability to feel, and the escalation of the horrors they perpetrate is only a measure of a more and more desperate attempt to rediscover that lost ability. But being in the presence of death itself carries both mystery and shock for us if we truly experience it, as, for instance, in saying a final goodbye to someone whose death is imminent, or in actually being there at the moment of death, or in the encounter with the unknown and unknowable in tragic deaths. Majesty and awe together, especially if the awe is religious, and if there is an element of dread, speak to this experience.

Both of these primary experiences, the mysterious and the awe-inspiring, point beyond ourselves—as it were, to the beyond as the foundation of existence.

Mythological Motifs of Opening

Part of our search for meaning is the search for our origin, our beginning. But beginnings are as something that is just "there," just appears, and origins are deeper than we can ever go. Our origins are numinous to us, hidden in both mystery and power.

Origins are openings, and in our search for the origins of consciousness, of light and seeing, and finally for the origins of seeing in depth, we may look for clues in mythological motifs of opening.

It is true that searching for the numinous in that beginning when we first discriminated opposites and attained ego-consciousness seems a paradox. What we call the clear light of our discriminating consciousness, the consciousness that separates a whole into its apparent parts, is a darkening of the light, at least of the holy light. As ego-consciousness develops, the holy becomes more dim and vague.

Nonetheless, the association of normal ego-consciousness with light is an important step in human development, and one that cannot be bypassed on the way to deeper consciousness, the consciousness that unites rather than separates the opposites. The separating consciousness is also experienced as numinous. It is the numinosity of rational discovery that drives science. That is to say, numinosity leads the way for us both in separating and reuniting.

Separation precedes reuniting as a wound precedes healing. The separation of parts out from a whole is thus a most purposive step in evolution, without which the reuniting would be meaningless. When something becomes "clear" to us, when we have an "Aha" experience, the power of separation is felt. We say that a light goes on in our mind.

As we have seen, the whole struggle of separation is portrayed in the myths of the world's cultures, in the image of the separation of the world parents, who are usually portrayed as Earth and Sky (or Heaven).

The Maori emergence myth presents the elements of the separation as related to the emergence of ego-consciousness most succinctly. In *The Origin and History of Consciousness* Erich Neumann describes it thus:

Heaven and Earth were regarded as the source from which all things, gods, and humans originated. There was darkness, for these two still clung together, not yet having been rent apart; and the children begotten by them were ever thinking what the difference between darkness and light might be. . . . They knew that beings had multiplied and increased, and yet light had

never broken upon them. . . . At last, worn out with the oppres-
sion of darkness, the beings begotten by Heaven and Earth con-
sulted among themselves as to what they might do, either to slay
or separate their parents.[2]

The children decided that the parents needed to be separated,
and after tremendous struggle, this was done. This myth is
quite clearly symbolic of the development of ego-consciousness, because the children are oppressed by darkness.

Ego-consciousness is mostly related to knowledge
based on differences or contrasts. Thus it is closely allied with
scientific knowledge. Our human curiosity is similar to the
urge out of which science arises. As noted above, however, it
is exactly the growth of ego-consciousness that begins to separate us from numinous experience and causes the loss of connection with the whole of reality from which we live, for there
are many different forms of consciousness available to us that
are not based in contrasts or opposites. Erich Neumann is em-
phatic on this point:

There are various forms of unconscious knowledge, and ego-
consciousness only represents one particular form of knowledge
whose clarity, precision, and applicability to the ego is dearly
paid for with its one-sidedness. . . . The fact that we associate
knowledge exclusively with the system of ego-consciousness is
the result of our obsession with the ego-complex, with which we
habitually identify our total personality.[3]

These other kinds of knowledge include knowing what we cannot explain to others, and the means by which our unconscious
formulates the symbolism of our dreams, and of myths such as
the Maori version of the separation of the world-parents. Similar to the organization of symbols is the unconscious knowing

by means of which our behavior is archetypally human behavior.

Another example might be our knowledge about future scientific discoveries. A primitive society, for instance, would not prepare its members to understand radio. Much preparation would be required: not only learning in our usual terms, but the development of the receptivity for the point of view within which such learning becomes possible. The very fact that there are always discoveries waiting for us in the future indicates an immense body of potential knowledge in the field, but the form in which it will come to contrast is not fixed.

Akin to this not-yet-contrast knowledge we must include the creative process itself. Often neither artists nor writers know immediately what they have created, nor do these creations all become rationally explainable over time. As Neumann says:

No matter how great the contribution made by the intentional work of the conscious ego, it is always surpassed by the creative process itself.[4]

Numinosity inheres in field-knowing (noncontrast knowledge), but fades as our rational understanding gains a grip on the material so understood.

To round out the point, religious experience and faith also tend to occur outside the bounds of contrast-knowledge, especially in such powerful experiences as a beatific vision.

Our lives now demand that we expand our consciousness in such a way as to enable us to join science and religion together again. We have already seen the paradox that a truer

Figure 5: Icon of Egyptian Separation Myth

consciousness includes the separating quality of ego-consciousness. We will see this theme again now.

The Egyptian version of the separation myth adds some important ideas to the Maori conception that can help us reintegrate our different ways of knowing. They are depicted in the icon shown in Figure 5.

The icon shows Shu, god of breath, holding Geb (Earth) and Nut (Sky) apart, raising Nut up with hands that also hold the sign of life, the ankh, and wearing the ostrich feather, symbol of the goddess Mayet, the World Order. Mayet is sometimes identified with Tefnut, Shu's consort. The whole scene can also represent an opening eye (another symbol of the emergence of consciousness), with Shu-Mayet as pupil, while Geb and Nut form the lower and upper eyelids.

Both the masculine and feminine dimensions are therefore represented in Shu, who is doing the separating. In the East, breath is associated with consciousness; development of deeper consciousness begins with deeper awareness of and practice with the breath. As Truth, Mayet also represents consciousness as a divine attribute. Breath symbolizes life and spirit, so that the separation of Earth and Sky is the work of deep divine purposiveness.

Matter (earth) and spirit (sky), the world-parents, must be separated if there is to be a "space" in which consciousness becomes possible. Ego-consciousness is simply the separating of opposites so that both can be seen—the same sort of separation depicted in the icon. In the Maori myth, the opposites cannot be seen for lack of light. As knowing by contrasts is the essence of science, knowledge thus attained is the root of our freedom. It is what we *do not* know that binds us. We are then left in the dark.

The Maori myth attributes the separation of the world-parents to the offspring of Earth and Sky, while in Egyptian mythology Shu and Mayet, who perform the separation, are the parents. Both views are valid. The Egyptian symbolism, of a pre-existing principle entering and transforming the Earth-Heaven pair once they have come into being, is beautiful, for it intimates that an intentionality toward consciousness is very deep in the scheme of creation. Finally, the Egyptian myth reverses the more common view that the Earth is feminine and the sky masculine. Again, both views are valid. The masculine and feminine each have an earthy side and a spiritual side.

In the Greek versions of our origins, earth and sky are originally one, but simply are separated in some unknown manner. Perhaps the most succinct telling is a fragment from Euripides' drama, *Melanippe the Wise:*

The tale is not mine, but from my mother, how the sky and earth were one form; and when they had been separated apart from each other they brought forth all things and gave them up into the light: trees, birds, beasts, and all things nourished by the salt sea, and the race of mortals.[5]

In Hesiod's *Cosmogony*, the oldest Greek writing on the origin of things, the first creation is, as F. M. Cornford interprets the writing, "a yawning gap between heaven and earth." He goes on:

When the gap has come into being, between the sundered opposites appears the figure of Eros, a transparent personification of the mutual attraction which is to reunite them.[6]

This reference to *eros* is the first concrete mention of love as a force in the whole process, and here love seeks the eventual reunion of heaven and earth, spirit and matter.

For clarity, let me reiterate the associations: Earth and reason (science) are contrasted with Heaven and revelation (religion). As the parents of consciousness, the sky (spirit) and earth (matter) together form a whole that gives birth to all of the diversity of life, including all the distinctions made by consciousness. As in the Hebrew Ten Commandments, both the father and the mother must be honored for us to have wholeness, both as individuals and in our culture in general.

In recent human history we have "honored the father," so to speak, and let the mother languish. On the other hand, as we will now see, they never were apart, except in our own perception.

Psyche

The space between the separated parents is where we live. In the Genesis story, this is called *raqia*, "expanse," most often translated by "firmament." Perhaps this translation reflects the mythologem that somewhere there are pillars that hold up the sky. In any case, it seems to correspond well to what I have referred to (in chapter 1) as the distancing, the standing back from a situation, that gives us space in which to reflect.

In the Chinese system, we saw that the "third primal power" is the human, which somehow appears between yang and yin, heaven and earth (chapter 3). We see the human as between heaven and earth also in the text of the Great Treatise within the *Book of Changes*:

Looking up, we contemplate with its help the signs in the heavens. Looking down, we examine the lines in the earth. Thus we come to know the circumstances of the dark and the light. Going back to the beginnings of things and pursuing them to the end, we come to know the lessons of birth and death.[7]

Here, the dimension of time is present also, and again the human is in between; in this case between the mysteries of beginning and ending, birth and death.

In this philosophy, as in others, the powers of spirit and matter gather at birth and separate at death to return to their sources. That is, the human psyche, or the human being, is something formed in the process of, and subsequent to, the separation of the original powers that provides the expanse, the place of middle being. If the primal powers, spirit and matter, had not been separated, they could not be brought together in parts to form finite individual beings. The Western, Christian cultural myth as well speaks of the separation of these parts composed of spirit and matter at death.

Psyche is not originally present in the dual powers of yang and yin, spirit and matter. It grows in the evolution of the whole. Our own scientific tale of origins agrees; originally there was no consciousness in the newly formed cosmos of the Big Bang. Now there is. The story of that consciousnessless beginning reflects the dream noted above:

In the beginning, in the small and the great darkness, life is not Something; it ardently Is.[8]

Gathering Consciousness

Consciousness arises as we gradually develop more accurate images of the world and of ourselves as part of that world, of how we have evolved with it from the beginning and were not placed upon the earth as a special creation. As we are now stressing, that accuracy includes the depths of reality, both inner and outer, and the depths of the psyche as well. The process by which consciousness arises thus applies to how we understand the universe scientifically, as well as to individual psychology.

Gathering consciousness is a process of taking ever more inside ourselves in a form as close to its own reality as we can manage. The continually increasing effectiveness of science in harnessing the powers of nature is the model of this gradual approximation to the way things are. Prior to every correction of our worldview, we think that the cosmos works in a certain way, which we merely imagine, or assume, based on less than adequate information. If our worldview had been right in the first place, no correction need have occurred. When we have seen how this process of gathering consciousness works with persons, we can return to apply it to science and spirituality.

Our unconscious assumptions that things, or perhaps certain persons, are what we falsely imagine them to be are known in psychology as projections. Our projections constitute our myth of reality. A person who is upholding standards might be seen as a tyrant, for instance; someone with whom we have fallen in love is erroneously seen as perfect in many, if not all, ways. The projected qualities are inevitably our own qualities, of which we have not been aware. These are often not quite savory qualities, but almost as often, they represent ways in which we could indeed act positively, if we could overcome our fears. When we accept the real situation as it is, which is usually a very difficult and drawn-out process, we say that we have "taken back" the projection, or that the projection falls away. If we truly "own," or admit to, the quality in question, we generally become better persons, as when we realize with humility that the tyrant image we had projected really describes ourselves instead of the other.

Let us begin, however, with infancy. The infant is in a state known as "infantile omnipotence." Since there is no ego, or "I," the infant identifies with totality, and if it is cared for, no correction to its view is needed for some time. Another term for this state is "the archaic identity of subject and object." This term is useful, for even when we are no longer infants, we assume, sometimes with a striking confidence, that the world, and especially people, are just what we think they are.

From an adult point of view, an infant is quite mistaken in its infantile omnipotence. From its own limited point of view, however, its attitude is justified by results, though it obtains those apparent results for reasons that it does not understand. When it cries, it gets attention, but not because it actually possesses godlike power. Generally, the growing child must learn many lessons as to the nature of the world before achieving the freedom that it begins to desire, once serious frustrations begin. Once the child realizes that much power resides outside itself, a process can begin by means of which the more it learns of the world, the more power for freedom it acquires. Cynically, we call this gaining of freedom "learning to play the game," but our freedom can also be used for genuinely helping humanity.

Our adult realization as to how the archaic identity of

subject and object operates comes through our observation that the growth of consciousness involves continual corrections to our understanding and our attitude. This alerts us to the fact that something general is going on, and gradually we learn to *assume* that we are under the influence of projections, and to be open to qualities that might surprise us, and to revise our opinions accordingly.

Children invest their toys, such as dolls and airplanes, with life and reality. One of the best recent popular portrayals of this investment was Bill Watterson's comic strip *Calvin and Hobbes*. When the six-year-old Calvin is alone, his stuffed tiger Hobbes is shown as living, playing, even fighting with Calvin; but when others are present, Hobbes is shown as a stuffed tiger. Many other devices are used as well to portray Calvin's imaginary world, most notably depicting him as a dinosaur or as "Spaceman Spiff." The contrast between these imaginings and adult reality often provides the punch line.

The child has some consciousness that a toy is inanimate, but Marie-Louise von Franz makes the important point that parents can no longer

join unaffectedly in play of this kind, because their conviction that the doll, say, is inanimate and the parent-child game is only fantasy *hinders them in acting out the game.*[9]

This observation gives us the needed contrast between the adult's point of view and that of the child. At the same time, we must acknowledge that we adults, too, invest imagined aspects of reality with life.

In cultures such as ancient Greece, "the whole world was alive with demons and spirits."[10] This sort of animism is well recognized as belonging to earlier periods of many cultures. And yet a higher form of the same spiritual investment gives much of poetry its power. Poetry is a doorway to the numinous, as is great music. The feelings that we get in nature, and the symbolic resonance of such things as storms, the rising and setting of the sun and the moon, the realities of deserts and jungles, and so much more, are a part of our very being at home on the planet. Life consists of these numinous experiences and is at the same time symbolically reflected in them.

There is an irreducible link between ourselves and our world, and in the end it is difficult to tell the difference between projections and real numinosity. Our only clue is our sense of the value of what we experience and what we do with that experience.

Psychologists think of projection mostly as a defense against insight, though not a conscious one. But projection is also generally the only possible avenue of new insight, for it is the Self's primary means of communicating with the ego. If we initially see ourselves in the environment, in sorting things out we learn both about ourselves and about the world. This process works to advance science as well as our individual consciousness, for our changes to our basic understanding of the world (e.g., in the work of Kepler, Newton, and Einstein) mean that we were seeing not the world but ourselves. The falling away of a projection (through the realization that one was wrong) is always a painful lesson for the ego, but without this pain, there can be no growth in consciousness. After all, defenses have their evolutionary value, too. When they are out of date, however, they become destructive in themselves. Adult defenses are ideally different from those of children, and mature defenses differ from those of adolescence, just as animal ferocity is no longer appropriate to an ordered society.

When we perceive something new, we feel an energy transfer, the resonance of what is new with what is known, as in the "Aha" experience. Beyond ordinary learning, however, we are also required to learn how to respond creatively to new situations, even to seek the unknown. To do this, we need to learn how to let the Self, which heralds the coming of a more comprehensive personality, lead the way in our lives. The Self wants opening and growth for each of us; it wants to show us the unlimited depth of life. For this to happen, we must break down our ego-bound intentions, our egocentric will.

The Self is the representative of the field, that is, of the whole of creation, in the individual (and beyond). The field and its patterning shaped the whole cosmos in its early evolution. The capacity of the Self to shape so-called external things can be seen in its ability to produce meaning through synchronistic events, which are its way of trying to awaken the attention and commitment of the ego. Such a commitment is not merely a yielding of the ego, but its recognition and participation in the deeper process that was always at work in the individual life.

The field always remains unbroken, even though contrast-knowledge has attempted to separate the inner and the outer. That is, we always remain connected to the whole of creation, in spite of our sense of separateness and our longing for autonomy. Freedom and autonomy can be ours, but not so as to violate the wholeness of reality. To say that we can only take the cosmos inside because it *is* inside, and not only symbolically, is to say essentially the same thing. Inside and outside are relative in the field. To speak of retrieving the energy that has been devoted to projection is to speak of letting the energy flow from the Self within, from the heart of the cosmos, from the heart of God.

The Role of Symbols

Separation precedes a reuniting that occurs on a deeper level, as a healed state is deeper than an unwounded one. The reuniting, or healing, actually establishes that deeper level. As a person who is healed is somehow more than one who was never wounded, a person who, like the "prodigal son" in Jesus' parable, has experienced separation and reuniting with respect to God, the Field, the Self, or other beings, possesses something that one cannot attain except in that way. As we saw in the Greek creation myth, the separation makes *eros*, attractive love, visible. In the separated world, love goes to work, to reunite that which has been driven apart.

That is, the activation of *eros* initiates a process of *gathering*. Love is the mover of all human curiosity and meaningful world-building, but *we* are the final products, as individually formed beings, because as we build the world, we build ourselves. We do this by assimilating meanings from all that we encounter as we live. We take the cosmos inside.

If we fail to do so, if we leave that which appears as outside ourselves "out there," we miss much. Perhaps letting God remain external to ourselves is the ultimate way in which we fail the divine presence in the world. The ungathered symbol blinds as well as enlightens, as is evident in the difficulty we have in seeing that it is indeed the Self at work, or, behind the Self, God, if we want to put it that way. The divine works within us by means of the love, or focused energy, with which we approach that which is deeply symbolic to us. At first we usually take a symbolic object at the face value of its attractiveness, before recognizing that something is trying to communicate with us through it.

While a particular symbol is active in one's life, one

needs no more, no further awakening, for the active symbol grants a sufficient sense of having been awakened. Great ideas, for instance, are symbols that channel the energy of great numbers of people, weld societies, and transform cultures. Examples are monotheism, monogamy, human equality, capitalism, communism, liberation of the oppressed, the apocalyptic view, the word, the great person, and science. Not all of these last, or have lasted, as values.

It is not the individual ego that is projected on the environment, but the Self, the archetype of wholeness and authority, and also the architect of our uniqueness in living. The ego usually remains unaware of the Self for something like the first half of life, unless something unusual occurs, such as a great hardship or tragedy. There is also no guarantee that the ego will become aware of the Self at all, for we always remain free not to see. Nonetheless, the process goes on whereby the contents of the Self are continually projected, and some of these are assimilated to the conscious person, if he or she is fortunate in self-discovery. As the whole cosmos is a symbol of the Self, so also the Self contains the whole cosmos within the person, at least in principle.

The round-about-ness, or involutedness, of the process whereby we come to deeper consciousness, if we will, is seen in the fact that the Self, as creative, inexhaustible Center, must speak to the ego through creation, that which is already there, i.e., external to the subject. In all the things we "must have," like cars, money, gadgets, and games, as well as in all that moves us in art and music, the Self is calling us to ourselves. Some of our responses are wounded, some more receptive of healing, but it takes so long to see that the grip of the object on our soul is not in the external thing. It also seems to take much falling in love to get past falling in love with ourselves (projection) to the point of actually seeing and loving another. The creation of ultimate importance is that of our own souls.

In calling us to ourselves, the Self is not finally working to build the ego, but rather the greater being that each of us might become, our more comprehensive personality, with our individual life-givens, in accordance with the view that we contain our own free destiny. The gathering itself is also the process of correcting our projections, our primitive assumptions as to the way things really are.

Symbols, then, are those images or objects through which the nonrational depths of reality speak to us. They always hold for us something more, something that will not be pinned down by our rational minds. They focus our psychic energy toward an inward, central goal, which is contact, and shared being, with the divine. The great world-myths are deep repositories of symbols waiting to help us to see what is most needed in our lives.

The fact that symbols do so move us is our continual reminder of the ultimate unity of spiritual and physical being. It is the still unbroken link with the worldfield.

Awakening to the love that is inherent in creation so that we can be helped in getting past ourselves, getting past our egocentricities to love other humans, is one of the most powerful saving elements in reality. That is, the other *as value* is one of the most universal symbols. But only when we cease to love ourselves in the object can we begin to see and love real persons and beautiful aspects of the world for themselves. Only when the ego has gained enough consciousness by accepting the hints of the Self can it sacrifice its claim to priority. Then we can gain the final freedom of living from a greater whole without worrying about material survival.

The opening of the eye, the separation of earth and sky, of matter and spirit, sets us directly into the field and flow of love, if we are open ourselves. But opening ourselves to the whole of reality is also what the opening ideally is. In the movement of the original opening of the "gap," the separating of the world-parents, it comes to light that the universe holds a separating push as well as a uniting pull. Between earth and sky, earth (matter, measurability), is the separating element, and sky (the atmosphere, spirit, breathing) is inclusive. How simple our lives are! We need food, we need breath, we need water; these three are symbolic of the triad of matter, spirit, psyche.

That is as far as the myth can go, in its collective form. The meaning is in the *details*, in all that is *individual*, in how each of us takes the path of love to our own wholeness. The meaning is in who we become.

CHAPTER SIX

The Cultural Path toward Convergence

Tell all the Truth but tell it slant—
Success in Circuit lies
Too bright for our infirm Delight
The Truth's superb surprise.
—Emily Dickinson

The past three centuries have witnessed the onset of rapid cultural evolution, including vast changes in the ways that we look at ourselves and our world. The process by which we have opened ourselves to new ways of seeing has deep roots, as we have seen; but the key to cultural evolution has been the explosion of knowledge, as science has come to adolescence. That is, science is growing with great energy, but still sees only a portion of the worldfield.

When James Burke opened his book *The Day the Universe Changed* by insisting "You are what you know," his forked tongue was probably in both cheeks.[1] Does the universe change, or do we? Burke was having fun with our pretentiousness at what we think we know. And yet, since there seems to be no cure for our sense of certainty, his joke is rather wry, and the truth in his opening statement is deeply ironic, since so much of what we know is so limited.

In any case, a crucial guideline in the process of knowing is to know *how* you know what you do, and not to go beyond that, if you can help it. So often, when a piece fits part of a puzzle, we assume that its placement has to be not only right, but final. Furthermore, when one piece of a given theory is corroborated, several other untested items also sneak into our assumptions about what has been verified.

All of us are enveloped—we might almost say trapped—in cultural views. Every one of us "knows" things that are not fully true to reality, whether these beliefs are religious in content or scientific. They are the things that everyone in a culture or group accepts without question.

We might well say that we are as limited by what we "know" as by what we do not, for if we assume we know something, we usually do not look for what we might be missing. On the other hand, there are indeed things that are known, and our images of reality do gradually improve. We know that because we discover ever more new phenomena that can be put to use, especially through science. In the process, we also discover where we had previously been wrong about the nature of reality.

Not only is our understanding of reality continually unfolding through discovery, but I believe that the process can continue without limit. Our universe is infinitely deep in all its potentials, including our understanding not only of physical reality, but of spiritual matters as well. A God whose unfolding had a limit, or final state, would be far too small.

The cornerstone of wisdom is, first, knowing what you *do not* know, but then knowing and acknowledging what you *do* know, which can also be difficult. Sometimes it is hard to face knowledge that is obvious to others.

When we thought that the world was flat, we would have asserted that statement with all the confidence of knowledge. However, a whole web of phenomena and measurements was waiting for our discovery and the correction of our error. Now we do know that the world is round. I have been arguing that we also now know that physical reality is nonrational, and that the general scientific attitude has been in error insofar as it assumes otherwise. In these and other such cases in which our knowledge falls short of the facts, I believe the limiting factor lies in unexamined cultural assumptions. We cannot progress much beyond our collective worldview at any given time.

Cultural change is a laborious process, for it is only through images that we have already received culturally that we can see anything new at all. That is, it is always the case that we already see things in a certain way, which seems to us to be the way things really are. An example previously cited is the evolution of the role of women in the twentieth century. In order for that role to change, we had to see the possibilities of the new through the veil of the old. As the images changed, we gradually became accustomed to a new seeing. Seeing the new through the old is a great paradox, of course, but however slowly and painfully, somehow it works out that we do progress in our ability to apprehend and comprehend ever wider realms as they come to visibility. As we will see, the themes and insights that open the doors to understanding can come from highly diverse sources. Perhaps that is even the case generally. The fact that clues to needed changes may lie hidden in odd places seems to be nature's way of tricking us into creative new ways of understanding our world.

If complementarity is a worldview, as I have described

it in the opening chapters, it can be generalized to include psychological and spiritual matters as well as physical. Then the fact that a single model can describe the nonrational unity behind all the pairs of opposites intimates that there may be a single center for all of the (ultimately inseparable) pairs of opposites and a single source-world behind all that we see. In the terms developed earlier, the *unus mundus* or unitary reality has a center that constitutes the center and origin of all of the opposites by means of which we see.

To move from a purely religious God-concept to one that includes science does not occur overnight. The necessary broadening of our outlook and our underlying concepts of reality has been in process for the past three centuries, from its early articulation by the scientist Emanuel Swedenborg. Through his spiritual opening, and without losing his perspective as a scientist, Swedenborg recognized the need for a complete and whole worldview that included both science and religion.

The whole cultural movement of the past three hundred years is, of course, a very broad topic. We will focus on the complementarity of science and spirituality as such, which is symbolic of the ultimate unity of matter and spirit, and we will further limit ourselves to a selection of participants in the drama, including especially Swedenborg, Søren Kierkegaard, some physical scientists, and Jung. Since the cultural evolution that is important here is essentially that from Swedenborg to Jung, it will be important to see their differences as well as their similarities.

Jung's work really holds the key to the present steps being taken toward unity of science and spirituality, for he described the psyche, which is the operative element that perceives the two as opposites, and that provides us with the images through which we interpret reality. Jung's psychology appears to be the only one that consciously recognizes the need to bring science together with spirituality, and the only one that attempts to honor both sides of pairs of opposites at all times.

The Swedenborgian stream that most informs me spiritually is not that of the various Swedenborgian churches, but rather the more general cultural influence that began with Blake and Coleridge, and continued through Goethe; Emerson; Carlyle; Henry James, Sr. and his sons; Robert and Elizabeth Barrett Browning; and Yeats, not to mention numerous artists and other writers.

Samuel Taylor Coleridge, for example, was introduced to Swedenborg's work by one of William Blake's later patrons, C. A. Tulk, an "adamantly non-sectarian Swedenborgian," who later also brought Blake and Coleridge together.[2]

That nonsectarian Swedenborgians took Swedenborg as articulating a paradigm, rather than enunciating "the truth," is evident in this quote from Coleridge:

By some hitherto unexplained affections of Swedenborg's brain and nervous system, he from the year 1743, thought and reasoned through the medium and instrumentality of a series of appropriate and symbolic visual and auditual images, spontaneously rising before him, and these so clear and so distinct as at length to overpower perhaps his first suspicions of their subjective nature, and to become objective for him, that is, in his own belief of their kind and origin,—still the thoughts, the reasonings, the grounds, the deductions, the facts illustrative, or in proof, and the conclusions remain the same.[3]

Coleridge's appreciation of Swedenborg's achievement is evident.

Probably the most important "visual and auditual image" Coleridge refers to in this quote is that of the central guiding figure of Swedenborg's visions, whom Swedenborg took literally as "the Lord Jesus Christ." As we know, Blake personified spiritual powers quite differently, as in the figures of Albion, Los, Enitharmon, Urizen, etc. I note this for the sake of those who may look into Swedenborg and be overwhelmed by the pervasiveness of the image.

Artists were attracted by Swedenborg's concepts of (1) "correspondence" between all things of the source-world and all things of visible space-time reality, and of (2) "influx" from the source-world giving life to the world of our concrete existence. Sculptor Isamu Noguchi referred to Swedenborg's doctrine of correspondences as a "universal rhyming scheme" by means of which all that is portrayed in art takes on definite spiritual significances.[4] That is, Swedenborg sees the spiritual world itself as the model and source of every visible thing—in detail. For practical spiritual purposes, the same is true of Jung's concept of the *unus mundus,* although for Jung the source of the correspondence is a spirit-matter unity (see chapter 1). Jung's position agrees with the model of complementarity.

However, both Swedenborg and Jung would agree with the psalmist when he says: "The heavens declare the glory of God" (Psalm 19:1). For the psalmist, the statement was probably a response to the majestic feeling of the sky of stars and planets. At any rate, it preceded not only the divergence of science and religion, but also science itself. For Swedenborg, who as a scientist was moved by the most minute aspect of nature, the divine presence in physical reality was even more palpable than the psalmist's sense of majesty in the remote skies. The idea of the divine presence at the root of physical existence, discoverable by examining matter scientifically, is the real opening of the present reconvergence of science and religion, though it is very ancient and has been with us all along.

Swedenborg and Jung

While Swedenborg was most important at the beginning of the modern reconvergence, Jung has been by far the most comprehensive figure of the twentieth century in the process. In the differences between the two, we will see more clearly the evolution of thought during the time between them.

Swedenborg himself can fairly be credited with initiating the modern convergence of science and religion. Because his lifelong interests were scientific, he saw the necessity for any theological view to accommodate itself to the findings of science as they became solid and trustworthy. For example, we have solidly established the geologic and astronomical timescale for the formation of planets and the evolution of life as taking billions of years. In response, thinking people no longer feel that the value of the Genesis account of creation is threatened by such facts; they see the account as symbolic of the evolution of the soul. However, it has taken a while to get used to that symbolism.

Just as Jung and Swedenborg differed in that Jung saw the source-world "as much physical as psychic" (or spiritual), so they also differed on the role of evil, or darkness, in creation.[5] These differences are in fact parallel, for culturally, Christianity has seen the material world as the root of evil. Swedenborg evidently thought so too, for Swedenborg's God is pure spirit and without darkness.

The source-polarity for Swedenborg was divine love and wisdom (see below), which contains no evil at all. For many Christians, evil is ultimately unreal, and is essentially

the absence of good. For Jung (and the present author), however, good and evil remain a pair of equal polar opposites that
follow from a deeper polarity, light and darkness, as consciousness arises in evolution. But, Jung does not identify light
with spirit and darkness with matter, for spirit and matter each
have positive and negative poles. The two polarities,
light/darkness and spirit/matter, form a quaternity.

Actually, Jung developed a much more complex system than this, taking all kinds of symbolic material into account. He even included natural numbers as a link between
spirit and matter, but it would be too much to go into all of that
here. He often referred to God as a "complex of opposites," but
he also emphasized the tendency of quaternities to emerge in
the human psyche as an empirical fact.

Jung takes the fact that such opposites as good and
evil are equally real in human consciousness as representative
of the nature of the source-world, at least in that one opposite
does not predominate over its mate. We have often seen that
qualities that possess the greatest reality to our conscious
minds merge in the worldfield, so that we cannot imagine them
as they are in themselves. It is very much as the psalmist de-
clares of God: "The darkness and the light are both alike to
thee" (Psalm 139:12).

Good and evil come to being with ego-consciousness.
We do not call animals evil that prey upon each other for food.
Only when there is conscious intent to harm or dominate others do we bring the concept to bear. In the realm of the divine,
the most we can perhaps speak of as originating there is "darkness" and "light."

Although Swedenborg did not include darkness in his
image of the Godhead, he did consider evil real, rooted in
human egocentricity, but which God "permits" for the sake of
freedom.[6] The fact is, however, that freedom comes only with

consciousness (see chapter 1). In Jung's view, consciousness is a central goal of evolution, desired by the source-world precisely for the sake of freedom. This sounds similar to Swedenborg's position, but it is subtly different. In *Answer to Job*, Jung concluded that the Godhead does not possess anything like our ego-consciousness, and that this lack is the ultimate motivation for divine incarnation,[7] a major difference that directly reflects the evolution of our cultural worldview. By Jung's day, the felt need for divine rational control had been greatly mitigated.

For Swedenborg, human freedom depends on an equilibrium between the good of heaven and the evil of hell. In his view, we are only able to act because this equilibrium is maintained by God for our benefit. In the worldview of complementarity, on the other hand, freedom is inherent in the nonrational nature of spirit-matter. Because he lived at a time when our present knowledge of the time scales of the evolution of life on our planet was unavailable, Swedenborg also was unable to take the evolution of consciousness fully into account. He also had not thought through the implications of his source of equilibrium, namely, that the earliest humans were not free, with no evil to counterbalance the good.

Of course, it is correct to say that they were not free, though on different grounds. The ongoing development of ego-consciousness that increases our freedom is a very slow process in human history. As Neumann said (quoted in chapter 1), to the extent that animals, including ourselves, lack ego-consciousness, they are "field-determined and unfree."[8] Julian Jaynes estimates that ego-consciousness only emerged about three thousand years ago.[9] The evolutionary view to which we have come in the meantime suggests a reason why humans might survive physical death even if "animals" do not—that is, because they have developed consciousness.

These are just some relevant examples of how the evolution of the scientific component of our worldview raised problems for the less conscious times in which Swedenborg lived.

The sections that follow cover other selected issues of cultural evolution that lead in the direction toward which our understanding is turning. The changes indicated have tended to move us toward freedom from our long-standing dependence on rationalism. They also have aided our gradual realization of the symbolic component in our interpretation of our world and of those texts that have been regarded as sacred scriptures.

The Divine Within

We saw above how Coleridge distanced himself from Swedenborg's literalism. This caution is a most important step in coming to real knowledge, as I said earlier. The same kind of distancing is evident in the approach to spiritualism taken by William James and Jung. Yet both approached it with openness.

In his *Memories, Dreams, Reflections*, Jung says that he read "seven volumes of Swedenborg" in a quest for material relating to the psyche, or soul:

Without the psyche, there would be neither knowledge nor insight. . . . The observations of the spiritualists, weird and questionable as they seemed to me, were the first accounts I had seen of objective psychic phenomena.[10]

Later, Jung read William James, and thus knew of James's involvement with the spiritualist investigator, Frederick Myers.[11]

In the conclusion of James's *The Varieties of Religious Experience,* Jung would have encountered the idea of the inner divine in the "subconscious self," of which he himself wrote afterward.[12]

It is interesting to note that this very central concept was introduced by Swedenborg sometime around 1752:

What principally disjoins the external man from the internal is the love of self; and . . . what principally unites them is mutual love, which love is never possible until the love of self recedes, for these are altogether contrary to each other. The internal man is nothing else than mutual love. Man's very spirit or soul is the interior man that lives after death; and it is organic, for it is adjoined to the body while the man is living in this world. This interior man, that is, the soul or spirit, is not the internal man; but the internal man is in it when mutual love is in it. The things that are of the internal man are the Lord's; so that it may be said that the internal man is the Lord.[13]

What Swedenborg calls the "external man," Jung would call "ego-consciousness." In Swedenborg's distinction between the "internal man" and the "interior man," we almost have Jung's distinction between the "personal unconscious" and the "collective unconscious," though the latter concepts are much more highly differentiated.

In speaking of such interior realities, Swedenborg also anticipates the description of "the within of things" given by Teilhard de Chardin in *The Human Phenomenon.*[14] Again, this spiritual core of every visible thing was what gave his writings so much appeal to artists.[15] Thus, Swedenborg's influence on the recognition of the unconscious was quite early, and certainly had a deep effect through the writers and artists mentioned earlier.

Universality

Perhaps the most powerful single spiritual thread in the cultural progress to the convergence of science and spirituality is the search for the most universal expression of the depth of reality. I am referring here to the simplest kind of statement or concept that encompasses the greatest amount of what we know.

Scientists have been searching for a single theory that can account for all phenomena, whether or not that quest holds any hope for ultimate success. Philosophers attempt to encapsulate their understanding of things in the simplest, most direct statement, such as Kierkegaard's "existence is contradiction," to which we will come below. Others, and here I include myself, search for that which expresses the depth in all religious or spiritual seeking and which transcends any given religious tradition. In other words, what is universal is that which unites humanity most deeply, and unites it most profoundly with our world and our universe. Swedenborg held that anyone of any religion who practiced that religion from a desire to do good was "saved." That is a profoundly universal religious outlook.

Here is an example of Swedenborg's influence in encouraging others to move toward the universal, which also ties in with the previous section.

When Henry James, Sr., the father of William James, was in the midst of a deep depression and was resting at a resort, he ran across a Mrs. Chichester, a Swedenborgian, who told him that he was experiencing what Swedenborg had called a "vastation," a purging or emptying of the things of self and pride. James had read an article by another Swedenborgian,

Dr. J. J. Garth Wilkinson, whom he then sought out in London. Among the works of Swedenborg that he then read was *Divine Love and Wisdom.*[16]

Henry James, Sr., felt that coming into contact with Swedenborgian ideas had rescued him:

It was nearly two years before Henry James, Sr., found substantial relief from his neurotic condition, but eventually he derived solace from Swedenborg's doctrine that God is not a personality but "infinite Divine love and wisdom" in union with the human soul; that Heaven and Hell are states, not places. . . . Henceforth James' religion was to lose every vestige of anthropomorphism and become completely spiritual.[17]

This is a clear example of moving toward the universal as a healing force in the life of Henry James, Sr. Incidentally, we also can see that the depression of Henry James, Sr., was instrumental in bringing William James into contact with the thought of Swedenborg, for his father went on to write many books containing his own formulation of nonsectarian Swedenborgianism. It also probably helped to moderate William's scientific temperament to be open to look at spiritualistic things, because he greatly respected his father, although they had many intellectual disagreements.

Complementarity in Swedenborg

In divine love and wisdom, we have Swedenborg's ultimate polarity. Swedenborg's treatment of this pair shows aspects of complementarity in that he refers to various opposites derived from divine love and wisdom as distinctly (or distinguishably) one. The first ten section headings of his *Divine Love and*

Wisdom illustrate his approach. The second five section titles are the ones that express the structure of complementarity:

1. Love is the life of humankind.
2. God alone, thus the Lord, is love itself, because he is life itself; and angels and mortals are recipients of life.
3. The Divine is not in space.
4. God is the essential Human.
5. Being and Existence in God-Human are distinctly one.
6. In God-Human infinite things are distinctly one.
7. There is one God-Human from whom all things are.
8. The Divine Essence itself is Love and Wisdom.
9. The Divine Love is of Divine Wisdom, and the Divine Wisdom is of Divine Love.
10. The Divine Love and Wisdom is substance and is form.[18]

There are over a hundred such headings in this little book. (Swedenborg did not present them as self-evident, but discussed each at some length.) Of those shown, the second to last shows the complementarity of opposites most fully, in the mutual reference of the poles. The last heading opens a discussion of spiritual substantiality, which is unlike physical substance, but completely palpable to spiritual beings. Swedenborg's "God-Human" or the "Divine Human" nature of God is shown here as well.

Among polarities, the masculine and feminine most show Swedenborg's complementarity. These have their deepest origin in divine love and divine wisdom, where the love (substance) is represented in the feminine and the wisdom (form) in the masculine.

In the next level "down" (so to speak) from the highest Godhead, the divine love is represented as good (feminine) and the divine wisdom as truth (masculine). In the third level, the outermost (as divine love and wisdom are the innermost), the original duality is shown forth as a pair of which the feminine is manifest as will and the masculine as understanding.

These levels are reflected in the psychic structure of humans. In Swedenborg's view, a male is outwardly an image of understanding, but more inwardly an image of will. The reverse is the case for the female. It is possible that Swedenborg's model of the inner masculine of the female and the inner feminine of the male gave rise to Jung's concepts of animus (the inner masculine in a woman) and anima (the inner feminine in a man), but we cannot assert it definitely. The model of complementarity is clear, especially in the added fact that, for Swedenborg, a whole human consists of a married pair.

The Uses of Understanding

As indicated in chapter 4, theological considerations dominated the early times in the history of higher learning. Even after science was recognized as a separate discipline, it was under great pressure to conform to ecclesiastical rule. To give just a few examples, Copernicus's treatise stating that the sun, not the earth, was the center of the universe was banned; Giordano Bruno was burned at the stake for insisting that truth is relative and that the progress of knowledge is therefore unlimited; Galileo was placed under house arrest and his writings were suppressed because he had asserted that the earth is not stationary, but moves. Even in our own twentieth century, Darwin's evidence for evolution brought vehement attacks from institutional religions, and universities were thought of as places where faith was destroyed.

In the first half of the seventeenth century, especially with the scientific work of Kepler, Galileo, and Descartes, a framework of fact began to be amassed that would ultimately reverse the domination of theology. The cultural motif that the earth was the place of imperfection and that everything "above" followed divine laws to perfection had held since Aristotle. In that view, the orbits of planets were held to be constructed on the basis of perfect circles. As we have seen, Kepler used the most accurate observations to date to demonstrate that no arrangement of circles could make up the orbit of Mars. In the process, he himself underwent an agonizing transformation of worldview in which he convinced himself that observation had to take precedence over theory. Galileo's telescope contributed to the downfall of the illusion of perfection above the Earth, by showing that there were mountains on the Moon, among other things. In this context, science and religion came to be viewed as mutual enemies.

Descartes had a more philosophical impact, along the same lines as Bruno, who had been burned when Descartes was four. However, he had different connections and made a better case, for Cartesianism, "freedom of inquiry," became the ferment of universities, where scientific and other disciplines sought to break free of tight church control. Swedenborg's own university career fell into these times, and he found himself at odds with his father, who was a Lutheran bishop and quite conservative.[19] The fact that Swedenborg's main interests were scientific was of undoubted importance in his mature view that individuals need to gather and assess their own evidence for what they believe, and that theology must assimilate what science discovers to be truly the case. Swedenborg insisted that only that which makes sense to your intellect and also elicits an emotional assent will be integrated into your life, will become what you really are. Heart and mind must agree.

When Swedenborg was at Uppsala University, by the king's decree every department *except* theology had been granted freedom of inquiry. In Swedenborg's later work, not only theology but every department of knowledge was open to his inquiry, as he followed what was to him an even higher decree. In one of his inner spiritual journeys, he was given the idea that led him to make one of his most famous statements: "Now it is permitted to enter with the understanding into the mysteries of faith."[20] We must understand this statement in the context of Swedenborg's insistence elsewhere that the emotional component must also be present before the integration of knowledge into one's life can take place. Not only is there no valid rote faith, but the intellect alone does not suffice for living.

Kierkegaard would agree.

Kierkegaard and Paradox

Søren Kierkegaard, champion of the "existing individual" and father of existentialism, accelerated Niels Bohr's understanding of physics by giving him the model for complementarity. This might be considered a most remarkable coincidence if it were not for the fact that the structure of complementarity is the same in so many areas of investigation. That is, that structure now seems to describe a general property of the universe: its paradoxicality.

In turn, Bohr, recognizing this universality, generalized the physics of complementarity back to the realm of concrete living.[21] Since Kierkegaard was a religious thinker, we can fairly speak of a spiritual influence interweaving with our understanding of the physical cosmos. And, of course, it is complementarity that Jung took as his own model of reality because it fit the paradoxes of the psyche that he was uncovering. In fact, complementarity is the most universally applicable model of paradoxical living that humanity has uncovered so far.

Swedenborg clearly saw that because the intellect has the ability to argue either side of a paradox, it can only be the heart or will that truly determines the state of a person's life. Kierkegaard deeply concerned himself with the same problem of paradox, but he opened up different aspects of it. Here is just one example, which holds parallels with what has already been said; for, of course, "paradox" is another expression for a nonrational union of opposites.

In a section of *Philosophical Fragments* entitled "The Absolute Paradox," Kierkegaard says:

The paradox is the source of the thinker's passion, and the thinker without a paradox is like a lover without feeling: a paltry mediocrity. . . . But what is the unknown something with which the Reason collides when inspired by its paradoxical passion, with the result of unsettling even man's knowledge of himself? It is the Unknown. It is not a human being . . . nor is it any other known thing. So let us call this unknown something: the God.[22]

Here we can intuit or feel "the God" as the hidden center of every paradox, and the paradox as revealing "the God."

Kierkegaard then speaks of the futility of trying to demonstrate the God's existence, precisely because the God's nature is paradoxical:

As long as I keep my hold on the proof, i.e., continue to demonstrate, the existence does not come out, if for no other reason than that I am engaged in proving it; but when I let the proof go, the existence is there.[23]

To let the proof go and trust existence is an example of what Kierkegaard calls "the leap." Here, the accommodation required of the intellect is accommodation to the Paradox itself, i.e., to God. As in Swedenborg, the masculine (differentiating) aspect must defer to the feminine (inclusive) aspect in order for us to live our lives. After all, the cerebral cortex, the organ of intellectual differentiation, is an appendage to the more interior parts of the brain where the emotional circuitry lies. Humans are primarily emotional beings.[24]

For Kierkegaard, *existence is contradiction*, which means that to be alive is to feel the pain of clashing opposites. For that aliveness to be real, however, one must continually open oneself to these contradictory aspects of reality. That is the definition of existential living, of which we can partake as long as we rely on our own inner nature for choice and do not go running to external authorities for answers. Jean Paul Sartre expressed the same idea in the saying that we are "condemned to freedom."[25] That is certainly the case if, as I have said, the root of our freedom is in the nonrational nature of the physical stuff of the universe. Again, we see the interweaving of spirituality with our understanding of the physical cosmos.

Jung and Science

We have followed threads from Swedenborg to Jung, both directly and indirectly through the James family. We have also seen, or at least pointed to, some general influences of Swedenborg on the whole cultural evolution down to our time, through artists and writers. In the process, we have seen themes to which Western culture of Jung's time was opening slowly, and which are still moving us now toward the reconvergence of science and religion.

Kierkegaard seems to be an independent source of the model of complementarity. His influence on the convergence of science and religion thus worked through physicists, especially Niels Bohr and his students. Of these, Wolfgang Pauli and Pascual Jordan directly influenced Jung. As I said earlier, Jung's importance lies in the fact that, as psyche unites spirit and matter, psychology has the potential to reunite science and spirituality.

The best evidence of what Jung thought of the relationship of psychology and physics is found in von Franz's contributions to Jung's *Man and His Symbols*, though von Franz is careful to attribute the similarity to the *Zeitgeist* and not to a direct influence of physics upon psychology:

Jung (working closely with Pauli) discovered that analytical psychology has been forced by investigations in its own field to create concepts that turned out later to be strikingly similar to those created by the physicists when confronted with microphysical phenomena. One of the most important among the physicists' concepts is Niels Bohr's idea of complementarity.[26]

She follows this statement with an accurate description of the wave-particle duality that gave rise to the complementarity concept. Going on in a similar vein, von Franz notes:

Bohr's idea of complementarity is especially interesting to Jungian psychologists, for Jung saw that the relationship between the conscious and unconscious mind also forms a complementary pair of opposites.[27]

Von Franz explains this in terms of the mutual interaction of conscious and unconscious. Now we have quite a universal model of the relationship of opposites in many fields, as Bohr envisioned would turn out to be the case, and which my own work has greatly substantiated.[28]

This unity turns on a more general relationship of spirit and matter. At the risk of being repetitious, I will again quote Jung's statement in "On the Nature of the Psyche":

Matter and spirit appear in the psychic realm as distinctive qualities of conscious contents. The ultimate nature of both is transcendental, that is, irrepresentable, since the psyche and its contents are the only reality given to us without a medium.[29]

Jung recognized that any truly radical monotheism must encompass both spirit and matter, the whole of creation, and explored that theme deeply throughout his therapeutic work and teaching.

But to return to the discussion in *Man and His Symbols*—von Franz offers a little more explanation:

No matter what we assert, we can never get away from the existence of the psyche—for we are contained within it, and it is the only means by which we can grasp reality. Thus the modern discovery of the unconscious shuts one door forever. It definitely excludes the illusory idea . . . that we can know spiritual reality in itself. In modern physics, too, a door has been closed by Heisenberg's "principle of indeterminacy," shutting out the delusion that we can comprehend an absolute physical reality.[30]

The work of explaining this situation so that we can grasp it with the contrast-knowledge of our ego-consciousness (as distinct from our nonrational knowing) has been undertaken by

Erich Neumann in *The Place of Creation*, his collection of essays on the worldfield.[31] (Some of the first essay was quoted in chapter 1.) Not only are spirit and matter unknowable in themselves, but even our highly functional duality of inner and outer cannot ultimately be sustained; it must yield to the wholeness that encompasses both inner and outer. The conundrum that God is within as well as without is thus resolved.

It is most appropriate that Jung, as an explorer of the human psyche, has been so instrumental in bringing science and spirituality together, for the psyche is what unites them in our consciousness and our deeper being. Ultimately, like inner and outer, and like spirit and matter, science and religion are two ways of knowing—of knowing the total unitary reality by contrasting means, furthering which has been the purpose of the model of complementarity since its origin.

We have seen Swedenborg's influence, not only directly upon Jung, but also indirectly by way of influences on Henry James, Sr., and William James. But above all, it was Swedenborg's insistence that the discoveries of science must be incorporated within spiritual understanding that marks him as the modern progenitor of the convergence of science and spirituality.

On the side of science, Niels Bohr, having derived the structure of contradiction from Kierkegaard (in the realm of spirituality), saw that complementarity could be generalized to life as a whole, and his later lectures were directed to presenting that case. It seems that we are almost ready to hear him, and to hear Jung as well.

CHAPTER SEVEN

Taking the Universe Inside

Understand that thou thyself art another world in little, and hast within thee the sun and the moon, and also the stars.
—Origen, Sermon on Leviticus 5:2

We have noted that while our experience of distinct realms that we term "outer" and "inner" is essential to living, the apparent separateness of the two ultimately does not hold. This situation is completely congruent with the structure of paradoxical thinking. Now we are ready to look more deeply at the relevance of this paradoxical structure of outer and inner.

Outer and Inner Revisited

The problems of living may be eased through our knowing that the presence of problems, in the form of struggling with the opposites, reflects the very heart of the universe. There is no rational solution to such problems; only living solutions that are unique to each case. As Mephistopheles says in Goethe's *Faust,* "To gain your end the act must be your own."[1] We must trust our own choices, without external authority. Emanuel

Swedenborg intuited this as well. We are just who we are, and all true paths begin with an honest acknowledgment of our own present loves and weaknesses. In any case, anyone who comes to grief having trusted himself or herself has lived well. Jung stated this with great force in the following, though we must note that by "barbarian" he means undeveloped, or one-sided. A major aspect of our one-sidedness lies in a tendency not to acknowledge our inner "beast," a part of what Jung termed our "shadow." Only a conscious completeness, a holding of opposites, confers true freedom. Only by integrating our "beast" into our consciousness (in accordance with complementarity) will we attain a true morality. Jung puts it:

We are still so uneducated that we actually need laws from without, and a task-master or Father above, to show us what is good and the right thing to do. And because we are still such barbarians, any trust in the laws of human nature seems to us a dangerous and unethical naturalism. Why is this? Because under the barbarian's thin veneer of culture the wild beast lurks in readiness, amply justifying his fear. But the beast is not tamed by locking it up in a cage. There is no morality without freedom. *When the barbarian lets loose the beast within him, that is not freedom but bondage. Barbarism must first be vanquished before freedom can be won. This happens, in principle, when the basic root and driving force of morality are felt by the individual as constituents of his own nature and not as external restrictions. How else are we to attain this realization but through the conflict of opposites?*[2]

Physicist Ilya Prigogine said essentially the same thing, when he noted that "an automaton needs an external God."[3] The whole growth of ego-consciousness, in which the urge toward scientific knowledge is a part, is motivated by a model of a feeling understanding as the goal of living. We want to know, but this must not become an end in itself. Rather, it must become a means to fuller being.

The convergence of science and religion seems deeply part of a process in which we can truly learn the nature of what is "outside" us only if we do indeed learn most deeply who we are "within." Paradoxically, we also cannot see the internal situation better until we see the world better. The Heart of the Universe, which we seek in questioning physical reality, turns out to have a deep connection with our own deepest heart of being. This is due to the fact that the distinction of outer and inner does not ultimately hold. Knowing that, we must hold the opposites together in our own being. We must balance the two paths, science and religion, outer and inner.

One aspect of this dual outer/inner journey is that we become ourselves, our unique piece of the whole, by a kind of opening of ourselves to take more and more of the universe in. This is an owning or admission of the subjective element in everything that we perceive as outside ourselves, even the stars, as asserted by Origen in the epigraph above. The other side of the process is an inward opening to see more and more of our inner being and depth. This kind of mutual self-arising is called a "bootstrap" process in physics.

Our ability to discern and understand physical reality deepens as our self-awareness or self-reflexivity develops, by means of which we distinguish "I" from "not-I." Thus, though this process does not represent an ultimate truth, it is, paradoxically, absolutely essential to the development of our consciousness.

As we have noted already, in the newborn there is no such self-reflexivity; rather, there is the "archaic identity of subject and object." The I and the cosmos are one, unconsciously. Edward Edinger describes this condition with respect to the inner archetype of totality, or the God-image within, which Jung called the Self:

In earliest infancy, no ego or consciousness exists. All is in the unconscious. The latent ego is in complete identification with the Self. The Self is born, but the ego is made; and in the beginning all is Self. Since the Self is the center and totality of being, the ego, which is totally identified with the Self, experiences itself as a deity. . . . This is the original state of unconscious wholeness and perfection which is responsible for the nostalgia we all have toward our origins, both personal and historical.[4]

Through experience, the ego emerges out of the Self as the person becomes more conscious in the process of concretizing her/his living uniqueness, known as individuation. Actually, the full process of individuation, becoming our deepest selves, involves both the original separation of the ego from the Self and the eventual relinquishing of ultimate control of the life by the ego, followed by its reconnection with the Self. This is fully parallel to the separation of science from religion, followed by the eventual turning of science toward the service of meaning and spiritual values. But there remains the deep truth of the original "archaic identity" to counterbalance the truth of individuation: all that is outside the being also is within, as Origen said. Or rather, our contrast-knowledge only illuminates the world like a narrow beam of light, while we continue to accept inner and outer as indistinguishable in many areas of living.

Since we begin life in a condition in which there is no distinction of inner from outer worlds, we learn only gradually to distinguish "I" from "not-I," first in a physical sense and later in a psychological sense. This includes learning that in many ways our inner world has a great deal of autonomy, and that there are inner "figures" whose actions and intentions are very like those of other persons, i.e., whose attitudes are unlike those of our egos. At first, we see other outer figures as judging us, or as carriers of wisdom, for example; we "project" our own inner negative judge, or our inner wise old man or woman, onto these outer persons. Often a great deal of emotion accompanies these and other projections. In order to retrieve our inner figures from being projected onto outer ones, we must learn a great deal about ourselves. We have an inner "family," and effective living with them can require give and take just as with our outer relatives and friends. This makes our task far from easy.

Projection Reconsidered

Whenever we think that a situation or another person really is as we imagine them to be, we are usually seeing only ourselves and not the true situation or other person. If we are lucky, our encounters teach us who we are as well as who others are and what the world is: We learn not to project our inner world onto the outer, but rather to see the outer more and more for what it is. This is an endless unfolding of knowledge, outer and inner. The point has already been made that the same situation is true in science, though usually the new, unfolded knowledge is more hidden.

In science, as in the personal examples just given, this weaving process of self-discovery and discovery of the other is equivalent to retrieving our projected selves and becoming more aware of ourselves as we truly are, not as we would like to imagine ourselves. In this way we are nourished by our environment and made strong.

Insofar as becoming ourselves is indispensable for our spirituality and religion, this process serves the spirit side of things, but it also yields concrete contrast-knowledge of the cosmos. This learning to know ourselves as we learn the nature of outer reality is the essence of science at its best. Knowledge of what the external world is like has enabled us to devote more of our energy to things other than drudgery. It has made a tremendous contribution to our freedom. What has been missing is the self-knowledge that would remind us of our inevitable subjectivity, and thus give us sufficient humility not to use scientific knowledge destructively.

The mutual self-arising of the knowledge of self and other, inner and outer, science and religion, and the permanent dependence of each member of each pair on the other is another case of a pair wonderfully figured in the ancient Chinese *t'ai chi t'u,* or Diagram of the Great Ultimate (see chapter 3). At the heart of the self is the other, and at the heart of the other is the self, and so on with the other pairs. Convergence is really a restoration of an original unity, but now with our awareness added.

Involution

A beautiful model for the process of taking the universe inside is to be found in our own physiology, in the early stages of our embryonic state, just after fertilization of the ovum. It is typical of the unity of science and religion that science gives us parallels to human myths, and vice versa, as we have seen in chapters 3 and 5, especially. In this case, we will be looking at a process that models *turning inward,* as well as *opening to the world.*

Potentially there is nothing outside that does not belong inside. Even God! The God-image inside is the Self, the archetype that arranges our world within, and brings us into contact with what we need to encounter in the world. The Self already bridges our inner and outer worlds. If we are to "take in" the world, we must become open in ways that we may well have not seen previously. We must be open to being nourished in new ways, spiritually.

Physically, taking nourishment from the environment is something we readily understand. It requires a bodily opening that is not, however, present at conception. The opening must be *achieved* by the new organism. This physical process carries a deep symbolic message for spirituality.

The process, known as "gastrulation," occurs in a wide range of animals from sea urchins to humans. In sea urchins (whose development is shown in Figure 7) it occurs within a few hours of conception, while in humans it occurs over a period of weeks. This process is the model for what I mean when I use the term "involution."

A fertilized ovum in the early process of cell division is living on food that was present in the fertilized cell, along with some oxygen from outside the cell for the "burning" of the food. This produces energy for the cell-division process itself. The tiny potential being is evolving, but using up its stored source of energy. Without a transformation of its mode of functioning, it could never grow; it would simply run out of energy. If it only went on dividing its cells, it would remain about the same size with an increasing number of smaller and smaller cells (Figure 7, steps 1 through 6).

Cell division thus cannot continue indefinitely. There is a limit as to how small a cell can be. How is the being to find a means of intake so that it can grow? It must undergo a total transformation of its way of being. It must become open.

Thus it "gastrulates" (Figure 7, steps 7 through 9). Cells that were originally on the outside are taken inside, involuted in a very literal sense. The growing being turns itself partially inside out to form an open system.

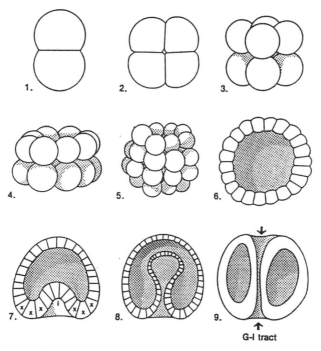

Figure 7: Development of Fertilized Ovum from First Division through Gastrulation. In the first stages of cell division, the cells simply get smaller. The process "runs" on internally stored energy, using a small amount of oxygen from the environment. At the eight-cell stage (3), the "blastula" is now fully three-dimensional, and thereafter develops into a hollow sphere (4, 5, 6). After the fifth picture, two or three cell-division stages occur between pictures, the entire depicted process requiring about a day. Pictures 6, 7, 8, and 9 are cross sections. In 7, certain cells' outer parts (x) expand, forcing a dimple or indentation (i) inward (8) until it meets the opposite wall and opens into a full gastrointestinal tract (9). What is shown as the upper opening (arrow) will become the mouth, and the lower opening (arrow) will be the anus. At this new stage, the blastula becomes a "gastrula" and begins utilizing energy (food) from the environment. This is a classic case of moving far from equilibrium to a point of instability (pictures 6 and 7, the formation of the indentation), followed by a reconfiguration that utilizes energy much more rapidly, which in turn begins a new move even further from equilibrium. The living entity is now much more engaged with its environment.

Another way to look at the process of gastrulation is that the embryo forms an internal tube, the gastrointestinal tract. The cells that have been taken inside the being are now in a different environment, which prompts them to begin becoming organs of digestion. Because cells are incredibly adaptable at this stage (another form of openness), they are able to change function. The being opens itself in response to the unavoidable pressures of the cell-division process (the impossibility of continuing indefinitely in that mode), and thus becomes able to take inside the food that was outside and make use of it for growing. This is physical nourishment, but the process is quite parallel to that by which we retrieve our psychological projections and are thereby nourished in psyche and spirit. The gastrulated individual becomes a being-in-flow, more intimately related to its environment. It is no longer a spherical protective shell.

The ego is, in some concrete sense, in a parallel position. It needs its closed spherical structure in the early, that is, immature, stages of its life. It needs to feel self-contained and in charge of its being (as in adolescence, whether confined to teen years or prolonged). But it too undergoes conflicting processes that entail an impossible (nonliving) outcome unless it can find a different source of nourishment. It too must turn partially inside out and open itself to form a spiritual "gastrointestinal tract." This turning is equivalent to *metanoia*, "turning around," or repentance. The partial involution, this inward turning, enables us to look to the depths within, from which comes the cry of longing for God. At the same time it opens the heart to that which is all around us, and refuses no event as a source of learning. Openness is thus as necessary for effective spirituality as it is for physical life.

Wherever a person protects something by holding back from risk there is an analogy to the pregastrulation cell-division stage. Living things need openness; without it they die. The parts of ourselves held back from living also die.

It is not often that we can see the true situation by ourselves, and as the cliche goes, "your best friends won't tell you." It often seems largely through some sort of grace—an accident, a slip, or the courage of a friend, along with a vulnerable moment on our own part—that we can come to the insight as to who we have been. That is very like the start of the "dimple" (the indentation, i, in Fig. 7, step 7) that will become the gastrointestinal tract. It is the beginning of an inward movement. In many cases it definitely involves a form of repentance for how we have behaved as persons in the past, but as we learn to open inwardly, we do so outwardly as well.

The cultural and religious beliefs with which we are socialized constitute the beginning of our shells. They do in fact "contain" us and protect us. Some of our original beliefs have to be transformed before we can let other ideas in, so the process is religious in an explicit sense, as well as in the discovery of meaning. Opening to the knowledge of humanity as a greater whole opens us inwardly to possible ways to respond to our religious emptiness.

Invented limitations are not the true limitations of living. Only with an opening up to what is not-I within and without can we find the banks of the stream of life that flows within each of us as individuals.

In order for the parallelism of inner and outer to be fulfilled, the scientific worldview must evolve to include spirit. This change will be as difficult for standard science as the corresponding move will be for established religion. Science must recognize that it has always gone beyond its ideal limits of measurability and quantification.

The evolution envisioned for religion is that it would open itself to see the divine in nature and in natural processes.

True to its etymological root as the binding back together of that which has become split apart, religion includes the task not only of binding science and religion back together, but also the binding up of a fragmented humanity, both individually and as a whole.

Gathering Inwardness and Consciousness

When a potential human is a fertilized ovum, it possesses, via its DNA, only bare information as to how to develop. It cannot be said to have an inwardness in the sense in which we usually mean that word. It has only a potential inwardness, which must be developed and actualized. At this stage there is almost none of the ultimate complexity of the fully developed adult. Virtually the entire universe, both materially and spiritually, is external to it.

The "blueprint" represented by the DNA of the newly conceived being is aimed at building the organism as a microcosm of the universe: as the Field constitutes the inwardness of the cosmos, the individual, as representative of the cosmos, must embody an inwardness to function as a receptor of universal experience. The human microcosm is somehow related to the whole, not only of human experience and its ancestral roots, but the experience of all living forms that share DNA—that is, simply, all living forms. All life is interconnected in its inwardness.

Through the gastrulation process, what was once the original single cell quite literally begins assimilating spirit-matter, nourishment, from its environment, which the DNA, along with the growth process itself, organizes into the body *and the inner being* of the child-to-be.

The growing being thus participates in what Teilhard de Chardin called "the within of things," a general tendency of living things to develop an inwardness, which is rooted, however, in the very nature of spirit-matter.[5] That things have a "within" means that nothing, least of all a growing being with a potential for high sentience, can be seen only as from without, as we might tend to perceive a brick, as an inert lump. I feel that in this concept Teilhard was sensing the meaning of the fact that anything at all can become a symbol to us; that it is in fact within us. That might be something like: to feel the inwardness of a stone is to feel the stone within ourselves, with a sensing function of which we are mostly unaware. However, for a being as completely egoless as is the embryo, or even an infant, that sense is completely immediate. It is the intimate connection that we really do have with all things, whether we know it or not.

The embryo already has a whole (unconscious) inner world that connects to the whole of the cosmos. Here I am referring to the symbolic fact that by taking part of its surface inside the growing being has opened itself to the nourishment available in the environment. Ingesting food is a form of introversion. By holding the foodstuff within, the nourishment may be drawn from it. What was foreign material becomes "me" through being broken down and restructured. It also seems highly symbolic that what was the external surface of the being becomes transformed to absorb this nourishment, when it is taken inside. This development of the physiological human also provides an analogy for the development of the conscious psyche.

Recollection

The consciousness of the growing human develops by a kind of reaction of the person to its own inner traits as seen in the surrounding world, which is called "projection" as long as it remains unconscious. A projection usually is accompanied by a strong affect, which can be extreme attraction or aversion to the object of the projection. If the person undertakes a self-examination as to the reason for the affect, this process leads, via recognition of the projected trait as one's own, to conscious owning of the trait and finally the recollection, or *ingathering* of projected contents. When self-examination of this sort is taken as a way of living, it leads both to a clearer seeing of what actually is "out there," and to the inclusion of wider and wider realms by the consciousness of the individual.

That is, in a sense the ego emerges by self-recognition, but it is ingathering that ultimately forms the deepest link of the individual with the cosmos. This fact has yet to receive serious recognition on any significant scale. What we have inside ourselves is what we can feel. If we can feel the humanity around us, we become human, and that on an ever wider basis.

Ego-consciousness is based on our ability to reflect energy from the stream of nature, and to form images that represent this stream to our ego-complex. As we look at things and situations, these images initially show us a tangled mix of ourselves and the world. A deeper consciousness is the product of a truer seeing, based on the work of owning and ingathering our projections—that part of our seeing that reflects our own state. It requires intensive work to develop our ability to open and transform ourselves thus. Marie-Louise von Franz speaks with wisdom when she refers to our mirroring of the world as a "mysterious quality of human consciousness."[6] The phenomenon is as replete with affect as a love story and as loaded with moral problems, especially when we are mistaking another person's traits, but also when we make blunders about what is happening. Situation comedies make full use of the lighter side of these errors of seeing, but the results can be tragic as well.

We have some models for comprehending the nature of reflection, but exactly how an image is formed, with the wholeness of the *gestalt*, remains elusive. Our self-awareness comes quite late in evolution, and then becomes so numinous to us that it occupies the whole field of attention. We come to it completely unaware that much, if not most, of what we see "out there" is projected. Growth in consciousness consists of taking inside what has been seen as outer. If undertaken rightly, this process actually fulfills Swedenborg's idea of renewal, which he called regeneration, the gradual building of a soul into a "heavenly" form, though in fact it represents a new being, not the restoration of a previous human condition.

Seeing

We see from within a cocoon, as it were, and the cocoon is our own existence as psyche, as vessels of reflexivity. Our typical form of consciousness is very much a product of our finitude and our mortality. We see as beings who will die must see. We are separate from the root-being of the cosmos, but that gives us the freedom to live or not to live in tune with the wholeness of the cosmos. We can sense the presence of our origins or we can hold ourselves aloof.

If we learn to see that every bit of what we think we objectively know is in part a bit of ourselves, we can be more serious, and certainly more humble, as to what we do with it. The same applies to thinking about God, of course. When Alexander Pope said that humanity is the proper object of study for humans, he understated the case.[7] Not only are we the only *proper* objects of our study, in a sense we are the only *possible* objects. But in studying ourselves, we find that we must include all other studies in the process. In sorting out ourselves from the cosmos in this manner, we learn about both; we improve our understanding of ourselves and of the world of our origins.

This duality of self-discovery and exploration of reality is part of *a universe that sets problems that only love can solve*. We are not given the capacity to uncover knowledge just for play, as if we were gods ourselves. The price of outer knowledge is self-knowledge, just as the price of aliveness is a transformation of our attitude. When we take in the universe *as a problem*, we really first encounter our true selves. And, in trusting ourselves, we will always be subject to error. Yet there is hope. As Jung said:

The right way, like the wrong way, must be paid for, and however much the alchemist may extol "venerable nature," it is in either case an opus contra naturam *[a work against nature]. [For instance,] it goes against nature not to yield to an ardent desire. And yet it is nature that prompts such an attitude in us. So it is as Pseudo Democritus says: "Nature rejoices in nature, nature conquers nature, nature rules over nature." Our instincts are not all harmoniously arranged; they are perpetually jostling each other out of the way. . . . Whichever course one takes, nature will be mortified and must suffer, even to the death. . . . No one . . . on the road to wholeness can escape that characteristic suspension which is the meaning of crucifixion.*[8]

We must undergo a death that leads to aliveness. Such is a theme that has been a major strand in western religious heritage—a theme that we must now begin to understand.

Dying and Aliveness

We have projected our aliveness onto a world beyond death, and thus continue to fail to find the meaning of living within ourselves. Our potential for aliveness thus remains unfulfilled. Finding it within does indeed require a death, but a psychic rather than a physical one. Jesus describes this when he says, "If you try to hoard your life, you will destroy it, but if you destroy the walls around your psyche instead, you will bring forth a flow of eternal aliveness."[9] The image that derives from this translation, which is actually more accurate than the usual, is a precise fit to the case of the embryo: we must become open in order to live, and open in a way we may not have yet imagined, to take in spiritual nourishment.

We have not learned to live freely at risk, and this fear of finding life within constitutes a fundamental fear of living. Jesus' thinking about this, however, is quite consistent with the knowledge that our spiritual aliveness is not the possession of our ego, but rather the aliveness of the divine within. That is what chokes if we protect our egos.

The ego must indeed die to the control of our lives, which makes attaining true aliveness a most arduous task. Aliveness does not flow like rain from heaven, but requires our fullest will and participation.

The rootless "mere-ego" feels that it must control everything in its life, especially all that represents a hazard with respect to its plans. It is focused on itself. When I function from my mere-ego, I unconsciously assume that my plans are what God would choose for me if God really cared about what I want. Most of us live in this manner some of the time.

When we care deeply about something or someone beyond ourselves, however, we will go directly into any danger to help the situation. We could hardly do this without some level of trust in the rightness of the total situation. We may succeed or not, but it is the right thing to do. These situations may well be our most spontaneous expressions of value, and our greatest aliveness.

Between these extremes of self-concern and spontaneous action on behalf of someone else, we might well learn to live more generally and fully in trust of the reality of the Field. Indeed, as we practice our awareness that our ordinary ego-consciousness is only a small portion of available awareness, there grows as well our openness to the possibility that we might be caring and planning in an ego-will mode, and that new directions might be open to us, and of greater value to the total situation. And so does our trust that something beyond us is guiding us for good.

In this regard, Erich Neumann reminds us that such has been the philosophy of Taoism for millennia:

One should think of the figure and teachings of Lao Tse, whose freedom from care means being free of an ego that clings to care and sorrow; it means open, carefree, spontaneity in harmony with the Tao. But even though we [say] that something within us takes care of us, that is actually not quite correct, for what goes on "within us" is not taking-care-of in the sense of human caring-for, but care-free caring. This care-free caring is the creative spontaneity that guides us. . . . When I am free of care, things flow by themselves: problems get solved, tasks are attended to, help comes. It seems as though the gates to the living only begin to open when I have drawn back the bolt of my care.[10]

For Westerners, the sacrifice of control is surely more difficult, for "self-reliance" has been a major theme of our history. However, I believe it is precisely what Jesus described as breaking down the walls we have constructed about our psyches. That death is the surest path to aliveness, for it permits us to attain a greater oneness with the universe. Teilhard said, "The universe is fundamentally and primarily *living*," so that as we take it in, we take in its aliveness as well.[11]

CHAPTER EIGHT

Religion: Binding Back Together

The conscious person is continuous with a wider self through which saving experiences come.
—*William James,* The Varieties of Religious Experience

In the word *religion,* the element *-lig-* signifies a connection; it can also be seen in our word *ligament.* Whether we say religion is binding things back together, or reconnecting, it is the same. We have become detached from our source, our ground of being, as Paul Tillich put it. Whatever helps us to reestablish our creative relationship to the ground of being makes up the content and meaning of the word *religion.*

This does not mean, however, that all of us must, or even can, establish direct, conscious contact with the unitary reality. The relationship in question comes in the form of our dedication to the pursuit of wholeness and openness in our own lives. We can assume a personal relationship to God by the way we live our lives.

Participating in groups formed for the purpose of mutual spiritual support is one way of approaching religion, but the spiritual well-being of the individual person is the goal of such associations. The primary indicator of their success is the kind of person that emerges from the association.

Whereas in Judaism, prior to the time of Jesus, the collective salvation of the "chosen people" seems to have been assumed, Jesus taught individual responsibility, as John the Baptist had done a bit earlier.

Another way to speak of religion is as healing the soul, binding up the wounds of existence. William James gave a very simple summary of the whole human religious endeavor near the end of *The Varieties of Religious Experience*:

It consists of two parts: 1. An uneasiness; and 2. Its solution. 1. The uneasiness, reduced to its simplest terms, is a sense that there is something wrong about us as we naturally stand. 2. The solution is a sense that we are saved from the wrongness by making proper connections with the higher powers.[1]

The fact that we have a capacity to be in touch with "higher powers" means that there is more to us than our ego, the part that feels the wrongness or incompleteness, and which also is the source of our healing, as James indicates in the quotation in the epigraph to this chapter. In another statement in the same section, James seems to point quite directly to what I have called the *worldfield*. He says that the higher part of a person "is . . . continuous with a *more* of the same quality [as our higher part], which operates in the universe outside of him."[2] It is not surprising, inasmuch as he was writing in 1902, that he places this quality outside ourselves.

Whether or not we join with others in some group devoted to our spiritual well-being is a matter of our aptitude to the spiritual journey and our choice as to the means for pursuing it. However, our relations with our fellow beings will always come into play. As Marie-Louise von Franz has put it:

What belongs to us is attracted to us. This means that bonds with other people are produced by the Self. One might describe this as the social function of the Self. *In this world created by the Self we meet all those many to whom we belong, whose hearts we touch; here "there is no distance, but immediate presence." There exists no individuation process in any one individual that does not at the same time produce this relatedness to one's fellows.*[3]

Contact with God reconnects us not only with other humans, but with the whole of the earth and ultimately the universe.

The Realm of God

The only sources that offer the possibility of discerning what Jesus might have said to his followers at the time that he spoke are the three "synoptic" gospels, Matthew, Mark, and Luke, for they clearly reflect different renderings of what had been given in earlier source documents, and thus one can compare the renderings and make substantial judgments as to the focus of each gospel writer. The gospel of John, not being based on those documents common to Mark, Matthew, and Luke, cannot be brought to bear in such a process, or only very sporadically at best. The important thing here is that thus it is possible to say with assurance that the writer of Matthew, when he found the expression "kingdom of God" in the source document that is closest to Mark, changed it to "kingdom of heaven," and where he found "God" it became "my father," when Jesus was speaking. Both Mark and Luke agree as to this, when all three are parallel. (For reasons of gender balance, I use "realm" instead of "kingdom" in this discussion.)

When Jesus said that the realm of God was within and among his hearers (Luke 17:21), he was clearly indicating that

that realm was not something that would come of its own in the future, but rather that it is actualized to the degree that we may take it upon ourselves to actualize it in our immediate neighborhood.

Though Jesus said that the way to enter the realm of God was to do the will of God (Matthew 7:21), there was no established authority to determine that will for individuals. How, then, was the will of God to be discerned? The only means at the disposal of Jesus' hearers would have been to act on the highest values that they could perceive. Among the values we consider would be those of our tradition, for it has been strongly influential in our becoming who we are, but this applies equally to the judgments of individuals with traditions other than our own. They would be doing the will of God as well, taking their own given values into account. Such a process is something with which it is at least possible for us to do our best. In working at doing the will of God, the ego takes its proper role as observer, evaluator, and servant of a deeper, non-ego process that appears to have its locus within us.

The realm of God exists wherever God is sovereign. At first this occurs within individuals, but then it can hardly help becoming interpersonal in form, because it leads us into better relations with our fellow humans. But what can this realm be, if God is beyond our ultimate grasp? Our participation with our whole being on behalf of the highest value we can conceive is the realm itself, because in our action God is sovereign to us.

This situation is precisely parallel to the case of science, in which the nonrational nature of reality forces us to enter the situation with our own personal commitment. It also echoes what Kierkegaard said about God as the Unknown engaging the passion of the individual (quoted in chapter 6). Wherever our ego-will defers to something greater than itself on the basis of values, we participate in and promote the realm of God.

The values in question will always evolve. This is one area to which ecumenical religious dialogue can contribute, particularly because the established religions distill the feelings of significant segments of humanity. However, the facts emerging from the scientific quest can also contribute by means of evidence about the whole evolutionary process, as we have seen.

The application of those values is in the area of the problems of living, including those of relationship, that have been given to us in our struggle to balance opposites. How are we to balance our personal needs against those of others? Shall we follow our hearts, or the demands of our society? What is the balance of emotion and reason in the case at hand? When shall we speak, when remain silent? How shall we balance our material needs against those of the spirit? When shall we follow the majority, when stand alone? When is mercy called for, when rigorous justice? Such are the issues that provide the conflicts that are the heart of literature and that reflect our own lives. These are questions that we face in many circumstances.

The opposites, split apart, become our frame of reference and our access to self-reflexive consciousness. As we work with them to become whole, we are, at the same time, binding ourselves back together.

Jesus characterized the realm of God as a "pearl of great price," which one could purchase at the price of all that we possess (Matthew 13:45–46). That pearl is precisely our singleness of purpose, or as T. S. Eliot put it, "a condition of complete simplicity, costing not less than everything." Kierkegaard made it the title of a book of meditations: *Purity of Heart is to Will One Thing*.[4] That one thing can only be the good, the highest value of which we are capable.

Forgiving the Universe

The transformations that are required of us in order to gain our wholeness, that is, to reconnect with the depths of our being, are not easy. Literature abounds with the insight that spiritual maturity comes at a "great price," as Jesus said about the realm of God. The phenomenology of the psyche gives us exactly the same message. Here is just one example, from Marie-Louise von Franz:

Insight into the nature, the essence, of the Self is purchased only at the price of great suffering that wipes out the worldly prejudices and preoccupations of the ego, thereby forcing it into a change of attitude. Every deep disappointment or disillusionment is, in this sense, a step forward along the way of individuation, if it is accepted with insight. . . .

When the suffering has lasted long enough, so long that the ego and its strength are worn down and one begins to feel oneself to be "small and ugly," then at last comes that merciful moment when reflection is possible.[5]

We see a flower grow, and we want life to be as simple as that growth, but our stage of evolutionary complexity no longer permits the "condition of complete simplicity" without our conscious participation, seeking a will beyond that of our egos. We have desires and aims that must be wrestled around to a direction that is not at first obvious.

We must struggle to be human, and for that, as for our relationships, compassion and forgiveness are essential.

We inevitably wound each other, and we are inevitably wounded by life itself. Humanity is a condition of being vulnerable.

Forgiveness is a wonderfully ambivalent word, for it can be taken as *forgive*-ness, the capacity to forgive, and also as a short form for forgiv*en*-ness, the capacity to accept being forgiven. This double meaning is essential to what I will be saying, for the forgiving life and the forgiven life are one and the same.

The Pain of Becoming

The world is not an easy place for those who see; those who permit themselves to see *feel the pain of human beings* (that is, have a sensitivity externally directed toward the lives of others), along with feeling the *pain of being human* (a sensitivity directed inward). However, the sensitivity to pain is the precondition for truly experiencing the joy of being, and the measure of the potential depth of that joy as well. The origin of that pain becomes an issue in living.

Those who begin to see eventually experience anger that things are as they are—that things are not usually solved for us by "God," that we must participate in our lives with all our being and courage. This anger then becomes the charge that brings us eventually to the need for forgiveness, in both senses of the word.

Pierre Teilhard de Chardin spoke aptly of the pain of becoming:

If everything in and around us is indeed moving toward a great union by love, the world should seemingly be bathed in joy. . . . On the contrary, I answer. It is just such a world that is the most natural and necessary seat of suffering. Nothing is more

beatific than union attained; nothing more laborious than the
pursuit of union.[6]

Teilhard gives three causes of this suffering. The first is our
lack of recognition of mutual belonging in spite of differences,
or, as he puts it, "unions missed, broken unions, incomplete
unions." The second cause of suffering is that

In order to unify in ourselves or unite with others, we must
change, renounce, give ourselves; and this violence to ourselves
partakes of pain. . . . Every advance in personalization must be
paid for: so much union, so much suffering.[7]

The third cause Teilhard calls the "pain of metamorphosis,"
symbolized by the fact of death and dying, but actually lived in
the process of our own growth. As he describes it,

No physical agent can grow indefinitely without reaching the
phase of a change of state. . . . On reaching a certain limit of
concentration, the personal elements find themselves faced with
a threshold to be crossed before they can enter to [the] sphere of
action of a center of a higher order. It is not only necessary for
them at that moment to rouse themselves from the inertia which
tends to immobilize them. The moment has come also for them
to surrender to a transformation which appears to take from
them all that they have already acquired. They can grow no
greater without changing. . . . *Deaths, death, are no more than*
critical points on the road to union.[8]

With this last statement, it becomes clear that Teilhard is not
speaking of physical deaths, but of all those psychological
deaths to which we are subject on the road to wholeness. It is
striking that Teilhard wrote these sentences half a century

before the science of chaos theory arose to offer and develop the same insights.

We often fail to see the necessity of this process, and so we turn toward anger because of the pain that we see and feel. It is this blindness and its consequent anger that make necessary the dual aspect of forgiveness.

When someone dies an apparently needless death, we tend to say that the ways of God are inscrutable. Let us look at what we mean when we say that, and what we are avoiding in doing so. In fact, we are avoiding an admission that the universe does not make mistakes. We say that "God's infinite wisdom" chose the particular time and manner of death, and that we cannot grasp that wisdom with our puny minds. This attitude seems duly humble in the face of divine mystery, but it actually amounts to turning away from the saving process of seeing and understanding what has occurred. The meaning of a supposedly meaningless death is not truly beyond our grasp, but grasping it requires us to break down the walls with which we protect our unconsciousness. The meaning of these deaths, if we had courage enough to look at it, would transform our lives.

The deaths that do not force us to revise our understanding of reality are not the really meaningful ones in the present state of the evolution of consciousness. That is not to say that a life fully lived is unimportant, but that the death with which it closes does not stand in the way of our celebrating that life or any other. On the other hand, the deaths of innocents and early deaths, seemingly random deaths through "acts of God," and death by suicide attendant upon a sense of failure, worthlessness, or the meaninglessness of suffering force us to ponder the values potentially inherent in creation.

When we are forced to change, we react with anger. This sets up the need both to forgive and be forgiven. We can forgive when we realize the ultimate goodness of the nature of reality, and we are forgiven when we move on in (into) harmony with that nature. Both of these require of us the courage to see the meaning of "pointless" deaths, and this in turn requires that we face the fragmentation of our own lives.

Centroversion

Forgiving the universe is a primary act in sacrificing the attitude of ego control, but it is also a central act of what Erich Neumann called "centroversion," for it permits us to feel more deeply, and to let the Center of centers grasp our being.

In defining centroversion, Neumann shows that he is speaking of the same general process as Teilhard:

Centroversion is the innate tendency of a whole to create unity within its parts and to synthesize their differences in unified systems.[9]

It is painful to perceive our partialness and inner moral conflicts.

What Neumann makes clearer than does Teilhard is that the very process of ego formation, which makes choice possible even though it clouds our perception of more subtle realities, is part of centroversion from the beginning:

The tendency of an ego-consciousness that is becoming aware of itself, the tendency of all self-consciousness, all reflection, to see itself as in a mirror, is a necessary and essential feature [of the process]. Self-formation and self-realization begin in earnest when human consciousness develops into self-consciousness. Self-reflection is as characteristic of the pubertal phase of humanity as it is of the pubertal phase of the individual.[10]

Thus through self-reflection the perceiving ego participates, or can participate, in its own process of unification, for that unification would be impossible unless we were able to see our own inner contradictions.

In our desire not to see our inner contradictions, we struggle to tread water above the depths within us. Only those who have seen enough to question the goodness of the universe and who have experienced the anger that results from that questioning come to the point from which forgiving the universe becomes a necessary and significant process. *We have to forgive the universe for giving us freedom and responsibility*, for that means that it is possible to fail *on our own*.

Those who too easily insist on a conventionally "good" God must force themselves to be blind to the pain inherent in our inner contradictions and in harsh mysteries such as the loss of those who die before their time. They do so because the notion of a difficult God that permits pain seems too heartless; such a God seems to engage in an uncompassionate testing of our courage to be. It takes a long time for us to see that this testing, including the possibility that lives can be broken off before an apparent consummation, is the very heart of compassion—that healing is the most profound fact of being alive, and that only woundedness makes healing visible. Only obstacles develop our creativity, which is another way of saying what Teilhard observed in the above quotations. The ultimate obstacle is the fact of our mortality, which is thus also the root of the fullness of our depth of being. We must forgive the universe for death, both universally and personally, for the fact of death itself pushes us to *live*.

Being Forgiven

Forgiving others and seeking forgiveness for ourselves is our field of practice, but it also is a concrete part of letting go of our anger at the woundedness of reality as a whole. Forgiving others makes us accept the fact that we necessarily encroach upon the world of others.

It is more important, though, to realize that living consciousness boldly (as distinct from living in unconscious boldness) is a consequence of *being forgiven*, that is, *living a forgiven life*. This state can be simulated by narrowing down the goals of wholeness within the framework of rigid religious beliefs, but that is not really the same thing, though it is of value. When we add the dimension of consciousness, rigidity of belief must be dissolved, which leaves us once again with ourselves in our uncertainty, as distinct from the certainty of unreflecting belief systems.

We may be *accepted*, but the difficult thing is to *accept acceptance in spite of unacceptability*, as Paul Tillich put it in *The Courage to Be*, which means a clear and balanced knowledge on our part that darkness is the root of compassion in the universe.[11] Participating in the forgiveness that we receive as part of being also deepens our relatedness to the Center of everything. This is centroversion, but it is initiated and motivated by the Center Itself. As was true of everything that we have been saying about the participation of our consciousness in the process, however, our acceptance of healing is as much a part

of binding things back together as the availability of the healing as such.

When we say that God is hidden and is waiting for us,
the place of hiding is the most profound imaginable: in the
depths of our own being. In creating a universe that is the
place of finitude, the full being of God, in fact, *must* be hidden,
but is nonetheless everywhere, in the within of things, and in
that which links all things in spite of separateness. God is
present without being graspable; God can be touched without
being bound. The venture into finitude for the sake of the possibility of reflexive consciousness is perhaps a form of death
for God, or maybe that is only a weak metaphor through which
we might approach such a mystery. Yet it makes possible a divine birth in each of us.

Human experience and testimony show that we *can*
participate in the depth of being; that is perhaps the only universal statement that can be made concerning the "design" of
it all. The principal hindrance to this participation is probably
our self-delusion that we are already doing so, based on some
system of thought or other. Of course we already *are* participating, but the process always needs to be deeper, and we tend
to be satisfied with ourselves at our present level of being.
Then the divine process must die again in us, or go dormant,
waiting for the next act of commitment. In order to move, we
must have compassion on ourselves for the fact of our obtuse-
ness in this regard, and on the universe for its harsh require-
ment, and just move onward.

We might say that the universe is hideously gorgeous;
it does not make mistakes. Our suffering has a purpose and is
the basis of all our life and joy. All the evil we have seen,
which we have felt would justify us in denying the possibility

of a good God, is material that we must assimilate to see the beauty! When we "forgive the universe," we really are becoming one with it, and we are also forgiving ourselves for holding ourselves back from the journey of deep living and of permitting the divine life to flow within us.

There is no concept of truly living that will square with a "fair" universe. While it is true that we all need to learn to live with each other, we are also enjoined by creation to follow our individual destinies. Even on its face this requires us to be open to the individual paths of others. Sameness is an initial state. If we were all truly open to the universe, our differentiation might engender less conflict than it does, but our difficulty in accepting our differences is not the deep source of the "unfairness" of the cosmos.

Rather, that source is the very limitation of each individual view of the world and the essential neededness of each. That is, the perception that the universe is unfair is a misperception. In the others in our lives and in the world in general, the opposites that make up God become visible. As J. Robert Oppenheimer put it,

It turned out to be impossible . . . for me to live with anybody else, without understanding that what I saw was only one part of the truth. . . And in an attempt to break out and be a reasonable man, I had to realise that my own worries about what I did were valid and were important, but that they were not the whole story, that there must be a complementary way of looking at them, because other people did not see them as I did. And I needed what they saw, needed them.[12]

Forgiving the universe is accepting our finitude and partialness and our own personal shadowy darkness, but it is also seeing ourselves as part of the whole, as one of many *needed* parts. Every human is in the same boat. Our help comes from others who have problems in the same way that we do ourselves.

And, for some reason, that is the way it was, is, and will continue to be intended to work. The universe sets problems for us that only love can solve.

CHAPTER NINE

Unity

We are much less afraid of the distant infinite than of the immediate infinite enclosed within ourselves.
—*Franz Werfel,* Star of the Unborn

The convergence of science and religion is not something that occurs in the realm of pure ideas, in the intellect alone, but occurs in the lives and hearts of humans. Both science and religion are about how to live as a part of the universe, in alignment with reality. At the same time, in the convergence of science and religion, the very concept of a universe demands the unity of God. We must take monotheism as far as it can go.

Looking at those whose focus has been primarily on either science or religion leads us to conclude that neither focus can solve all of the difficulties encompassing the whole of life. Those focused on religion may neglect the substance of what we know about the cosmos and how that affects their belief, while those focused on science may neglect spirit altogether. This situation in itself shows the human need to bring the two paths together. Neither science nor religion can be whole without the other, nor can we be whole without incorporating both to some extent.

The wholeness or completeness of individuals is not

all that is at stake, however. What we need, in this time of external economic, ethnic, statistical-political, and religious determinism, is to bring what we all would call a deeper humanity to our dealings with each other. To do this we need openness and compassion.

Let us look at each a little more closely to see what might be different under the influence of the worldview of complementarity. First, we will look at science.

Alienation and Involvement

Our ultimate choice is to be ourselves or not, which now includes our depths. Another way to put it is that we must bear the burden of the divine, or turn away from it. None of our knowledge *forces* us to become a living part of the whole patterning of the cosmos. We do so out of our freedom, but it is not an easy burden to take up. Openness never was easy. It is easy to see the darkness only and demur. As I have suggested, I have a different perspective on it: the universe sets problems for us that only love can solve.

When we awakened to the possibilities inherent in our consciousness, the opposites were born. There love was also born as a possibility (remember Hesiod's account in chapter 5), a love undertaken freely because we see the beauty of creation—not the beauty just of external nature, but of this whole experiment in darkness and light. A paradoxical reality is the greatest gift God can give, for it is precisely the gift of freedom.

And, once we have seen the depths, it will no longer do to live superficially, as if our ego-consciousness were all there is to us.

Scientists may be very involved with the meaning of their work, but standard (rationalistic) science does tend to cut off our avenues toward a sense of a pervasive meaning for life. The lack of a sense of meaning that encompasses our lives is a potent source of neurosis. We tend to feel that our retreat into the security of what is rationally known is wise; but an inner dull ache, or even an anxiety, remains to remind us that what we have shrunk ourselves down to by retreating is not all that there is to us. Here is an example from Steven Weinberg's *The First Three Minutes*:

The more the universe seems comprehensible, the more it also seems pointless. But if there is no solace in the fruits of our research, there is at least some consolation in the research itself. . . . The effort to understand the universe is one of the very few things that lifts human life a little above the level of farce, and gives it some of the grace of tragedy.[1]

If the "point" of the universe lies in the spiritual realm, there is no way that the methods of standard science might reveal it. Only one who has thrown out the baby with the bathwater, who has judged all of spirituality as a lesser pursuit, would be in such despair. And despair it is, though it may feel heroic to stand defiantly at an empty shrine and challenge the emptiness to battle, as Weinberg does.

The ego-consciousness of a scientist, or anyone else functioning in the rationalistic mode, is a diminished form of consciousness, which Erich Neumann calls the "mere-ego":

The philosophy of rootlessness so characteristic of our times is the philosophy of an ego that also suffers from megalomania. It is rootless because it speaks as a "mere-ego" only for itself and knows nothing of its connection with the Self on which it rests, from which it springs, out of which it lives, and which remains indestructibly present in its own numinous core.[2]

The megalomania lies in the rational ego's insistence that it, using rationalistic logic, is the sole arbiter of reality. It must fail, and thus it must despair. Interestingly, rational theology often finds itself in the same situation.

Neumann also says:

As a "mere-ego" we are encapsulated and imprisoned, and the Western rational ego is just such a poor, crippled mere-ego. But that is not sufficient reason for cursing this mere-ego, or, like the East, wanting to be rid of it. This poor ego also needs comforting. It must be told that as a mere-ego it is not itself. For not until we experience ourselves as a Self-ego *do we arrive at what we are. The mere-ego exists in anxiety and despair. . . . Even the mere-ego crushed by concentration camps, by hunger and torture, and hurled back into pure creatureliness remains a divine being, descended from the divine and belonging to the divine.*[3]

How one can convey this knowledge, this deep inward feeling, to one whose life has been devoted to the rational is not easy to discern. Only one who begins to feel that something is missing or wrong will be open to listening. Often it takes some kind of severe emotional blow, but that is not our present task or topic.

The new possibility for the convergence of science and religion *in us* is based in part on an aspect of complementarity that addresses this issue of alienation directly. It is known in physics as *the essential involvement of the observer in what is being observed*. We have noted that by the very structure of reality we are called upon to enter the situation with choice and intuition (chapter 2). This is a direct contradiction of the erstwhile ideal of science, of which Einstein was a great champion, namely, absolute objectivity in the form of removing the influence of the experimenter from that which is studied. Symbolically, the ideal of science has been precisely alienation.

Part of the needed transformation of science is looking newly at the very meaning of the word *involvement*. We not only must choose; we must care, just in order to see. It is certain that if we do not see creation as beauty, we do not see at all. If we are open, it draws us into it. Again, this is a lesson from science, from complementarity.

This is hardly obvious to the rational mind, being contrary to the usual assumption that we only see well if we are detached. It is, however, the appropriate way of seeing the situation in a cosmos that seems to be "designed" to promote the spiritual as well as the mental well-being of its inhabitants. God is not disclosed to the dispassionate. If the universe sets problems for its creatures that only love can solve, as I have tried to show, caring is only an initial step.

Of course, nothing can force anyone to care about things. I believe, however, that everyone does care, somewhere in their humanity, however deeply it may be buried. Caring has been seen as part of the spiritual side of humanity. It is only as we integrate science with spirituality that it becomes a common aspect. It is humanity itself that becomes the focus, to be approached by either or both of the two paths.

Things that come in the form of hard evidence do not require anything of us. In that sense, sticking to hard evidence is safe. These are the things for which science does indeed function in its accustomed mode. On the other hand, *requiredness* is a deep human experience that makes us feel that something is demanded of us by existence itself. Such an experience makes us feel anything but safe, but it contributes greatly to our aliveness. Physicist Ilya Prigogine, a pioneer in chaos theory, expressed the same thing when he said, "Good physics is physics that does good."[4] That is a profound sense of involvement.

In looking at science and religion as transformed under the vision of complementarity, it becomes harder to tell them apart. Both involvement and the acknowledging of meaning move science a step toward the traditional turf of religion. On the other side, the recognition that physical reality is part of the fertile ground of revelation means that science can no longer be undertaken as a neutral quest. There are spiritual implications hidden in all that we come to know. If we are to live with integrity, our integrity must include both intellectual and emotional aspects.

Thinking about God

Twentieth-century science, by providing the groundwork for the paradoxical nature of reality, has finally opened the door to a truly radical and inclusive monotheism. Since the first emergence of a secular world (see chapter 4), there has always remained something that we have held back from the divine realm. The unity of science and religion means that a final synthesis of the secular and the divine, but now a conscious synthesis, has appeared as the goal of human evolution, just as the unification of humanity on our planet now appears as the goal of cultural evolution.

The earliest clear emergence of monotheism may be the Sun worship instituted by Akhenaten in Egypt, around 1350 B.C.E. There is considerable evidence that this monotheism was the religion of the pharaoh's brilliant mother, Queen Ti. It may well be that Akhenaten desired to unify all the religions of his kingdom in the form of an abstract and ever-present deity, which was nevertheless freely available to all in the openness of the divine self-presentation. The notion that God either is, or appears as, the Sun, is not in itself rare, but here was an early attempt to establish a single deity as the source of everything and governing all aspects of living. Even physically speaking, all energy other than nuclear that has ever benefited humanity has come from the Sun.

The fact that monotheism was introduced in Egypt at the time of the Hebrew captivity was probably of great importance in the evolution of monotheism within Israel later. Several psalms have distinct Egyptian links, and one is virtually a translation of one of the early pyramid texts. One of the most interesting of the pyramid sayings has to do with both Hebrew and Christian scriptures: "Thou art my son[, my beloved]; this day have I begotten thee." This is echoed in Psalm 2:7 and some versions of Luke 3:22.

From the sun as god to God as something like the sun, that is, as imaged in and through the sun, is a great step. The question always arises, however, as to how universal any given concept of God may be, how inclusive of all divine attributes. The step from God as super-human, to God in a human form with attributes illumining the divine through such capacities as love and intelligence, for example, is similar to moving toward symbolizing God as the sun. It speaks to us deeply, but there is always something more that we feel of the divine that has not been included in any image.

On the other hand, to say that the divine is beyond all imaging leaves us with nothing through which we may satisfy those concrete happenings that evoke our thanks and praise.

Unity and Wholeness

Our search for God has been much like the early Greek thinking about the single originating element, whether it was fire, or water, or whatever. The attribution of supreme importance to one single aspect of reality, or super-reality, is known as henotheism. One can focus on a single attribute and have a *unified* God-image, but if the God-image is to be *whole*, it must include all that humans (at the least) have felt as divine.

Henotheism is very much like single-issue politics, in which social justice, or personal freedom versus the sanctity of biological human life (as in the abortion issue), or the rule of law, or the welfare of labor becomes the absolute focus of one's vote. Those devoted to single issues are often very noble and do much good, but it is always to the exclusion of some other issue to which someone else might be equally devoted. Single issues never encompass the whole. With regard to the image of God, some single-issue foci might be God as spiritual only, or as external to ourselves only, or as masculine only, or omniscient in the sense of ego-consciousness, or omnipotent, or as all light, without the balance of the opposites of these qualities.

One path from henotheism to monotheism, the belief that there actually is only one God, is to ask what is the most inclusive image we can come up with. Each of the attributes just mentioned has an opposite that has also been attributed to God at some time or other. Since we have seen how pairs of opposites make unities, this inclusiveness also increases the overall unity of our image of God, in acknowledging a divine source for both sides of each pair. William James refused to believe that there could be any source of darkness in God and that therefore God was most likely plural and finite.[5] In the present view, that would be a diminishment.

In approaching monotheism we must also ask how

much of the world's religious thinking can the God that we are imaging encompass. It is certainly the case that world-religions have envisioned different images of God, while yet claiming to be monotheistic. They have also generally assumed that their own particular version of the divine was superior to those of other religions. To move beyond this situation, we perhaps need first to commit ourselves to openness as to how to conceive of God, for at least the reason that serious and good humans have had different ideas about it. If there is only one God, that must be the God of all being. How adequately do we conceive this God? Is it really likely that the vision of God found in any given religion is the final one?

We must recognize that any and all particular conceptions of God must always remain at the level of belief, even though powerful personal experiences may move us to conceive God in one way or another. They may reflect our personal knowledge, while not attaining to the status of universally recognized knowledge. Our beliefs, however, may nonetheless be informed, or reasonable, beliefs. We work to make them so.

One might well say, if there are no objective proofs regarding the nature of God, then why bother believing anything at all? One answer is that we have certain experiences that we do in fact share with other beings, at least insofar as we are able to communicate them, and that our common human feeling leads us to see beyond ourselves to a creator, at the least, and so we move from there to a vision of various attributes, in accordance with our experiences. We have much in common. (Perhaps the still foremost document of such experiences is to be found in William James' *The Varieties of Religious Experience*.)[6]

Another answer, particularly relevant here, is that we are recognizing that we have no proof of the ultimate truth of our scientific concepts, either, yet we use them effectively in our living. Part of that usefulness lies in the fact that our scientific experiments do *exclude* certain options, and we may reasonably function in the same manner in thinking about God. For instance, to return to the example of the crystal spheres supporting the planets (chapter 2), as our spacecraft moves from Earth to Jupiter without any hindrance, any belief in the crystal spheres that might remain tends to fall away.

Since there is no proof for God's existence in general, we can hardly assert particular attributes. What we are concerned with, then, is the quality of our beliefs, and how those beliefs fit in with what we know about reality. Our reason is free for any use to which we may put it, including thinking about God.

We also need to remember that the very image of reality is evolving continually. Still, it is important to have some sort of "working image," or model of God, and to reason about what might be the case, based on that image of reality as a whole. All we can do is give our best thinking to our concept of God.

Radical Monotheism

In an attempt to open and expand our thinking, James Fowler gave the following description of what he calls "radical monotheism," a concept that he credits to H. Richard Niebuhr. This will give us an excellent place from which to begin to push our understanding of God to a new level. He says:

Radical monotheism implies loyalty to the principle of being, *and to the* source and center of all value and power.[7]

Fowler notes that one need not even conceive of this principle and source as God, or as divine, and that it certainly is not limited to Western forms of religion. Buddhism, for instance, is a nontheistic religion to which it can equally apply.

One of the great values of conceiving religion in this way lies in the fact that every concrete religion thus becomes relatively valid, as distinct from any having a claim on an absolute truth. Religion, like science, then becomes an eternal progress toward truth and understanding. In this way, too, religion and science become more truly a complementary pair, in that they are more alike, more parallel.

One of Fowler's characteristics of his "primary principle and power" is that it is necessarily transcendent, by which I understand that he thinks of this principle and source as nonmaterial. This is one respect in which I would want to go deeper.

The unity of spirit and matter, in their complementary nature, means that we must learn to understand differently the nature of what we have called physical reality. If there is no matter without spirit, complementarity would seem to require us to see somehow that there can be no spirit without matter. Here we are reminded again of synchronicity (see chapter 1). Physical events also are carriers of meaning. The whole of creation is an expression of God's physicality, the capacity for finite form.

The world is definitely a place that the spiritual puts to use, and not only by revealing to consciousness the nature of the divine. It is part of the fullness and unity of all that is, and its central purpose seems to be that it is the primary vehicle for the evolution of reflexive consciousness, even for the self-awareness of God, to speak in those terms.

The following came to me some years ago:

The God of spirit-matter is not a God who is the spirit in matter. The substance of God is Holy Spirit-Matter.

The expression "Holy Spirit" has been used enough that the sense of discontinuity in saying "Holy Spirit-Matter" may be evident.

How does one put such a concept of God into practice? Two of Jung's statements have a bearing in this area.

We live wholly when, and only when, we are related to God, to that which steps up to us and determines our destiny.[8]

And,

I do know that I am obviously confronted with a factor unknown in itself, which I call "God" by universal consensus. I remember Him, I evoke Him, whenever I use His name. . . . This is the name by which I designate all things which cross my wilful path violently and recklessly, all things which upset my subjective views, plans, and intentions and change the course of my life for better or worse . . . a "personal God," since my fate means very much myself. . . . Yet I should consider it an intellectual immorality to indulge in the belief that my view of God is the universal, metaphysical Being of the confessions or "philosophies."[9]

These statements are practical as well as personal. It seems easy to "believe" in the higher ideas of God, but in fact we all, to some extent, recognize that material events are not excluded as meaningful. This is clearly recognized even in law, where the term "act of God" is familiarly applied.

A form of radical trust is required of us if we hold that we are where we are as part of a cosmic whole. This is not a version of the old determinism that said that some were born to be gentry and some to be servants. That view also held that disease and death were meted out as the cost of sin. This view is not at all concerned with one's relative position in society, but with what one can accomplish where one is. The approbation or opprobrium of others simply does not count, or rather it counts only to the extent that it counts with the individual, when one lives solidly within oneself.

Another area is opened by this statement of Fowler's:

Radical monotheistic faith calls people to an identification with a universal community.[10]

While I feel that what I have presented agrees with this quite completely, our conception of that community can still be very divisive. How inclusive is our image of humanity? Whom or what do we exclude in our feeling and concern? Could we welcome in our hearts, first, those of other religions, but then also other species in the universe with whom we might communicate? Where do we stand with regard to criminals, to those with mental debilities, and so forth?

My own criterion, which I follow only haltingly at my present stage of maturity, was first stated by the Roman poet, Terence: "I am a human; I consider nothing human alien to me."[11] When I run into those whose attitudes seem reprehensible to me, I must stop and ask what atrocities I would be capable of committing. Yes, there are those whom it seems to me we could easily do without, but there are none from whom we cannot learn something of the range of human capacities and appetites. *If we feel that they are alien, we do not know ourselves deeply enough.* Only when we are aware of our dark capacities can we hope to protect others from our own evil. Jung stated this beautifully:

It appears that men cannot stand me in the long run. Since I do not deem myself god-almighty enough to have made them other than they are, I must put it down entirely to my own account and lengthen my shadow accordingly.[12]

That is, he recognized that the negative effects that he had on others were his own responsibility. That is a step that few of us generally take. Of course, there are much deeper forms of evil than our everyday failures in relationships, but the cumulative effect of these has a devastating effect on society as a whole. Everyday living is where we are most intimately ourselves or not ourselves.

We really know that there is no unmixed motive, method, goal, or outcome in terms of good and evil, and that "good" persons are not withheld from their evil, but have learned to deal with it by facing and transforming it. Like First Man in Navajo mythology, they can say, "I am filled with evil; yet there is a time to employ it and a time to withhold it."[13] People struggle with their choices of action, wanting the best outcome for all concerned, but not knowing either that the result of their choice will be the outcome they imagine, or, even if it is, that one outcome will hold more good than the other. That is in God's hands.

Radical monotheism acknowledges that darkness is part of the wholeness of creation. The lodging of life in finite forms is itself a dark act on the part of the divine, since it introduces death and suffering, at least, but in no other way is divine self-reflexivity possible.

Religious Pluralism

A little over a century ago, an event occurred that became, in the title of a book about it, *The Dawn of Religious Pluralism.*[14]

The event was the World's Parliament of Religions, and it was a part of the Chicago Columbian Exposition of 1892–1893.

Under the generally difficult conditions of global travel at that period, representatives of many faiths, including a dozen or so major world religions, journeyed to Chicago to represent and discuss the nature of each of these religions and their effects in the lives of their adherents, including their cultural influence through art, literature, commerce, law, and social life in the places where these religions have their homes.

Among those who came first to America under this call was a young student, D. T. Suzuki, later a great interpreter of Zen Buddhism to the West, but then the language interpreter for his own Zen master, who had been invited to the congress.

Although by today's standards the participation of women was small, in terms of the culture of the day, it was of breakthrough proportions. As the organizer of the parliament later declared, "Never before did women have so large and noble a part in a series of religious assemblages."[15] In fact, they had their own parallel meetings, but for its time it was a great step.

The proposer and organizer of the parliament was a Chicago attorney, Charles Carroll Bonney, who had developed a deep conviction of the universality of religion out of his study of Swedenborg. Swedenborg's position was that each person whose intent was to do good from the sincere practice of religion was "saved," whatever that religion might be. To me, this is one of Swedenborg's great contributions to the expansion of our idea of God.

If we follow that path, we also must try to imagine how it might encompass all of the creatures that surely inhabit the visible universe. We must ask what doing good is, apart from any written code, or any historical event, or purely cultural considerations, for instance. And we must also recognize that there is an infinite variety of forms that valid religion (as a human way of healing what is divided in us and as a way of experiencing reality) may take.

Two statements of Bonney's give concrete expression to these principles. One was given to the opening session of the whole parliament, and the other to the first of its meetings, which happened to be the Jewish Congress. We will look at the latter first. The language is that of the time, but amended now for gender neutrality.

MASTERS AND TEACHERS OF ISRAEL: OFFICERS AND MEMBERS OF THE JEWISH DENOMINATIONAL CONGRESS OF 1893: . . . We know that you are Jews, while we are Christians and would have all be so, but of all the precious liberties which free persons enjoy, the highest is the freedom to worship God according to the dictates of conscience; and this great liberty is the right, not of some only, but of all—not of Christians merely, but of Jews and Gentiles as well. I desire from all other persons respect for my religious convictions, and claim for myself and mine the right to enjoy them without molestation; and my Master has commanded me that whatsoever I would have another do to me, I should also do to him or her. What, therefore, I ask for myself, a Christian, I must give you as Jews.[16]

It seems strikingly apt to find a validation for religious pluralism in the teachings of Jesus. However, Bonney's more general statement of religious pluralism occurred in his opening address to the whole assembly, which we pick up in midstream:

Let one other point be clearly stated. While the members of this Congress meet on a common ground of perfect equality, the ecclesiastical rank of each, in his or her own church, is at the same time gladly recognized and respected, as the just acknowledgment of his or her services and attainments. But no attempt is here made to treat all religions as of equal merit. Any such idea is expressly disclaimed. In this Congress, each system of religion stands by itself in its own perfect integrity, uncompromised in any degree by its relation to any other. . . . Without controversy, or any attempt to pronounce judgment upon any matter of faith or worship or religious opinion, we seek a better knowledge of the religious condition of all humanity, with an earnest desire to be useful to each other and to all others who love truth and righteousness.

To this more than imperial feast, I bid you welcome. We meet on the mountain height of absolute respect for the religious convictions of each other; and an earnest desire for a better knowledge of the consolations which other forms of faith than our own offer to their devotees. The very basis of our convocation is the idea that the representatives of each religion sincerely believe that it is the best of all; and that they will, therefore, hear with perfect candor and without fear, the convictions of other sincere souls on the great questions of the immortal life.[17]

Of course, respect does not imply the absence of challenging dialogue. It is *listening*, in particular because we recognize our own need to be challenged, and that ideally our views are actually fluid; though no one may offer a real challenge, someone might. To respect another is to expect the highest and best, and to accept no less. The essence of science is challenging criticism, just as the essence of journalism is asking the hard questions. If we focus on respect and discussion, we bring the best of science to the religious discussion.

These guidelines bear much study. A worldwide religious movement need not bring everyone to identical beliefs. If anything, a conviction of the unity of opposites presents a wider range of religious expressions that can be held and lived with integrity than a rationalistic worldview could ever hope to do.

Bonney's principles of plurality are remarkably prescient when we consider that virtually the whole development of modern psychology has taken place since the time that he articulated them. In the following comments on how the archaic identity of subject and object (see chapter 5) works in interpersonal relations, von Franz makes essentially the same points:

When unconscious identity operates negatively it causes us, naïvely and thoughtlessly, to take for granted that the other is like us and that what is valid for us is also valid for the other, so that we feel justified in "improving" the other, that is, in raping the other psychologically.

The inner mental image must be recognized as an inner *factor; this is the only way in which the value or energy invested in the image can flow back to the individual, who has need of it for personal development. This difficult moral task makes it impossible for any relatively conscious person to want to improve other people and the world.*[18]

That is, knowing ourselves and accepting our own worldview as our own without forcing it on others is the basis for a true human pluralism on our planet.

God's Long Loneliness

The assumption of humanity as a special creation, added in a completed state to a previously completed world, still pervades philosophy, law, theology, and science (see chapter 1). One way I have found to combat my own unconscious assumptions in this area is to think about the whole long evolution of life while also thinking about the divine at work in the process. Not only are we a product of that long co-evolution; our engagement with it shapes the outcome in the most profound ways.

We are enjoined by the process of discovery in which we are eternally engaged to employ our best thinking in the service of aligning ourselves with reality. That includes our attempt at the fullest theology consistent with everything that we know with reasonable certainty. The entrance of the intellect into the inquiry is not neutral at all, but changes the picture, "co-creates" the picture of the world, including our ideas of God and how the field brings about the evolution of forms. That, in turn, shapes how we live. The fact that intellectual inquiry will take its own course, and that that course will shake up the theological realm, is only to be expected. Science will evolve and move the foundations of faith in the process.

Here again we touch on one of the most potent conclusions of science: the evolution of consciousness from unconscious stuff (spirit-matter) over the past fifteen billion years (see the Appendix). This process has no conceivable end. Because our ability to see reality as it is increases through time, we are forced always to reassess our understanding. This brings the whole enterprise to life.

The open-endedness of evolution really follows from the nonrational nature of physical reality, for if there is no final rational formulation, there is no end to the process of complexification of neural systems, interweaving of awareness, and refinement of sensibilities. It is probable that, in the future, there will be a state of consciousness generally available to which ours will seem like that of the blue-green algae that dominated the earth for billions of years.

What was the status of the developing cosmos during the first few billion years? Was God "waiting" for humanity to appear? Was God active, interested—in the blue-green algae?

Was the not-yet-human "Lucy" (*Australopithecus Afarensis*) part of an ancient "church"? If anyone survives physical death, there had to be a first such being. At what level in evolution might this have occurred? Did it emerge with the genus *homo?* With the essentially modern Neanderthal humans? Thinking about such things is much easier with a "special creation" of humanity. Then all the questions are eliminated, and life is easy, not to mention death.

In view of the facts of evolution, it seems clear that our God-image needs rethinking. God must be a full, active shaper of the whole at all epochs in the cosmos, drawing each step forth, and each step being of unimaginable consequence.

What about individual species—for instance, the tree-shrew that was our ancient parent? Species come and go. In what, then, might God be interested? Species beyond ourselves are to be expected, and might even be in process of emerging at the present. I find that I can only take these views, however, if I consider that the same evolutionary process is proceeding on into the indefinite future, i.e., for far more than another fifteen billion years. Perhaps God is not waiting for anything specific to emerge, but is eternally surprised by the events within creation.

Although it could be that God is still waiting for something more interesting to emerge, I like to think that God is awakening; that our self-reflexive form of consciousness is newly available to the divine self-awareness. The idea that God's consciousness is new and growing accords with the above picture of evolution and begins to make sense of many issues in theology that are problems only when one assumes that we live in a rational creation.[19]

I want to close with the ending of a poem by my friend and mentor Sheila Moon. The poem is called "Conversations on the Son of Man," and is a trilogue involving Jesus and the prophets Ezekiel and Daniel. Ezekiel argues for the Son of Man as a *tremendum*, the power of God transforming the world; Daniel speaks to a sustaining inner strength and stillness; and Jesus to the experience that follows from a response in love to a divine call, such as he experienced at his baptism.

My own studies of the Synoptic Gospels have led me to the conclusion that in the figure of the Son of Man, Jesus was referring to a new birth within humanity in general. That new birth is indeed our connection to the divine, which moves us to incorporate our response to God into our own lives.

It may somehow be salutary to the soul to disclaim all movement or activity in our own spiritual renewal, but I feel that now we must take upon ourselves the courage to forego the disclaimer. Centering, or the establishment of equilibrium on the basis of an intent to act upon the highest value we can discover in the total situation, and weighing choices that are each potentially the highest value outcome, is something we undertake, but which is also part of our surrounding, cultural and otherwise. The stirring within, as well as the arrangement of the outer situation, is the work of the divine, but it also defines the human. The total outcome is "co-creation," in which our seeing and intentions play a part.

Jesus speaks:

God's long loneliness,
seeking since Adam to father love
equal to creation, becomes a Son of Man
wherever we will take him as a work to do.
Few will. Few care to shoulder God,
to lift burdens of forgiveness,
or choice, or unsheltered journeys
to painful dawns. Few dare to swallow

Jonah's black waters. When you do—
O Ezekiel, then truly the Son of Man
is a ripe storm! And still as a seed,
Daniel, small as a mustard grain,
with myself, ourselves, humanity's self
the fertile, lightning-ploughed sprouting ground
for God's becoming.[20]

The Anthropic Principle and the Web of the Universe

The word *universe* is a promise, or hope, of a wholeness that contains and relates all that is to be found within the cosmos, visible and invisible. It asserts the ultimate unity of everything. In this context, the word *invisible* refers to that which ultimately cannot be shown, but which nonetheless is inferred on the basis of things that can indeed be seen. The invisible includes the essences of things as they are in themselves, and much of the vast field of all that we know nonrationally.

In building a view of "the universe," we are actually building in ourselves a container that can hold together all that it is possible to experience. That is, we must experience deep changes in our psyches in order to see the universe more as it is.

However, as we fit phenomena into a unified world view, we also build confidence in the actual unity of the whole.

Until now, life has not been a part of the universe! Rather, it has been seen as a special creation, distinct from physical things. The fact that the exclusion of life (by standard science) has not seemed absurd is itself testimony to the power of the psyche to see things in its own way, for whatever reasons, religious or political. In fact, it is still difficult for scientists to see life as originating within a merely physical ground.

The Anthropic Principle is an attempt to correct this oversight.

Consciousness

The cosmos is diverse and certainly contains at least apparent contradictions. Yet we still postulate a universe. In spite of so many opposites, we still feel that there must be a unity. Our science gives us strong indications that the same physical laws hold throughout, which is reason enough to search for the unity behind the visible reality. We are looking for the web of the universe; that which holds it all together.

We live in a cosmos that contains both matter and spirit. (We will acknowledge the presence of spirit even if that makes scientists uneasy.) The equal reality of opposites in one thing makes that thing complete, or whole, yet not without conflict. Our human consciousness, at least, feels a conflict between the matter and spirit sides of our being. Often a wider conflict between the matter and spirit aspects of existence itself is felt as well.

It is the spirit aspect of the cosmos that makes life and consciousness possible. Fifteen billion years of cosmic evolution after the origin of the cosmos in the "Big Bang," the cosmos now contains that which physicists call "the observer," and which Jung called the ego. This identity of ego and observer is important because of Jung's definition of consciousness:

By consciousness I understand the relation of psychic contents to the ego, insofar as this relation is perceived as such by the ego. Relations to the ego that are not perceived as such are unconscious.[1]

That is, consciousness is predicated on the existence of an ego and the ego's awareness. For Jung, consciousness is not a term to be applied to an overarching principle of existence itself. The congruence of Jung and physics will be seen more fully as we look at the Anthropic Principle.

Matter, spirit, and ego-consciousness, then, are salient components of the cosmos, corresponding to the fields of physics, spirituality, and psychology. Jung forcefully makes the point that we cannot understand either science or spirituality until we understand something of the psyche; we do not know the *thing-in-itself*, because all the images or *gestalts* that we have of things are already within the psyche:

It is an almost absurd prejudice to suppose that existence can only be physical. As a matter of fact, the only form of existence of which we have immediate knowledge is psychic. We might well say, on the contrary, that physical existence is a mere inference, since we know of matter only insofar as we perceive psychic images mediated by the senses.[2]

Moreover, not even *thinking as such* can grasp the thing-in-itself:

Thinking is after all a psychic activity which, as such, is the proper study of psychology. I always think of psychology as encompassing the whole of the psyche, and that includes philosophy and theology and many other things besides.[3]

Matter and spirit have often been regarded as strange partners, inspiring many attempts at a reconciliation, at least in our understanding. But *as we know them*, both are contained in the psyche, which is the inner aspect of the web of the universe. This is, of course, not to say that the psyche contains them as they are in themselves. On the contrary, we have good reason to suppose that they are trans-psychic realities, reaching beyond the realm of our comprehension. To repeat, though, we know them only from within psyche.

The interweaving of science, psychology, and spirituality has a history of excellence. Wolfgang Pauli, one of the great physicists of this century, whose "exclusion principle" provided the physical foundation for the understanding of chemistry, collaborated with Jung, whose work revealed unprecedented depth in the human psyche, and has provided a foundation for the understanding of spirituality as a human phenomenon. My own work builds upon this collaboration in the sense that I continue the interweaving of science and psychology, but I also indulge an interest in new religious paradigms.

Let me begin with a diagram, shown in Figure App.1.

The arrows assert a continuity from the origin to the present time, which means that spirit, life, and consciousness represent a development from within, not something "stuck-on" later. Another way of putting it is that we physicists seek physical solutions to cosmic presences. Thus physicists have come up with the Anthropic Principle, which asserts this continuity: The physics of a cosmos containing conscious beings must be such as to permit (engender) life and consciousness. That is, physics must finally permit itself to be critiqued on the basis of the presence of life, spirit, and consciousness in the

Fifteen Billion Years
Big Bang **Now**
Matter: **Spirit:**
Simple Elements -------> **Life**
Unconscious --> **Consciousness**

Figure App. 1

cosmos, and must change in cases where the critique shows previous physical concepts to be inadequate. The discussion of the Anthropic Principle indicates a need for new openness in the scientific community.

The Anthropic Principle is currently studied by numerous physicists. In December 1991, an eight-page article appeared in *The American Journal of Physics*, entitled "Resource Letter: The Anthropic Principle." It had 142 entries, including 6 books devoted to the subject, and chapters in many more books, besides the usual journal articles.

Physics Reexamines Itself

The Anthropic Principle is based on the continuity of evolution. Physics naturally proposes physical explanations for phenomena. This stance would force us into the error of viewing life, intelligence, and spirit as supernatural. Since the initial and present states of the cosmos, as indicated in the diagram, are considered to be well-established, continuity demands that we discover how to see spirit and the roots of consciousness as present at the atomic level, i.e., to see that atoms and molecules must be viewed as what Pierre Teilhard de Chardin called spirit-matter, and thence to trace the links of the primordial cosmos to present beings, with their human spirit and religious dimension.

The work done in this field impinges on the conceptual foundations of physics. The conceptual area links theory and experiment and is insufficiently studied, perhaps because most physicists lack philosophical training. Our physical concepts are hard won by long study and contemplation of phenomena. For example, what we now call "energy" was once called "living force." It took a great deal of experience with the phenomena to separate out what we now conceive energy to be.

There is something refractory about even our simplest concepts. For example, momentum is mass times velocity, but what are mass and velocity? Both of these concepts involve our notions of space and time, which we know are inadequate as they stand, and so forth. Theoreticians tend to use a symbol in a certain mathematical structure to stand for the conceptual quantity and simply trust it, as it were, for all time, which is not at all assured.

We have seen throughout this book that conceptual analysis shows that the phenomena of physics are fundamentally nonrational, and therein lies the conflict with traditional views. Physics has shown that such elementary things as electrons and photons must be described by employing logically contradictory concepts, if the description is to be complete. Physically, an "electron" is both a wave and a particle, i.e., it is both continuous with its surroundings and discontinuous, which are logically contradictory attributes. What, then, is the completeness of the electron? We can only imagine such a thing as a unity of opposites that lies in some manner behind the electron's manifest properties.

In general, most scientists have hoped for a rational world. Physics has shown that the world is not so, and we must follow the findings of physics against those scientists who feel a need to hang on to a rationalistic worldview. As a note to this, logicians are disturbed by the notion, valid in logic, that if two contradictory assertions are both true, then all assertions are automatically true. The implied objection to the discoveries of physics would have real weight if physical reality were rational, but it is not. One can only insist on rationality at the expense of reality. But then, recall the saying that is found in all three of the synoptic gospels: Matthew 19:26, Mark 10:27, and Luke 18:27: "All things are possible with God," which is hardly a rational assertion. If *God* is real (and not rational), why should the *world* be rational? I do not mean this face-tiously in the least, but as a reflection of God's beauty. Our knowledge that the cosmos is nonrational makes room for God. One might even say that it draws God in. If "all things are possible," the fact that as far as we know, all things do not happen certainly points to a kind of limitation in nature, but not to its rationality. We cannot expect pure logic to explain the World-Order of a nonrational cosmos. That is why physics will always be fundamentally experimental in nature and finally insoluble from a purely theoretical point of view.

To summarize, the first holding together of the cosmos is the recognition of continuity in the evolution of the cosmos. Since we find matter, spirit, and consciousness within the cosmos, the latter increasing with time, we recognize a process that leads from an initial state of the cosmos to the present state, tying matter and spirit together. Needless to say, I see the deep unity of creation that is revealed as a source of the most intense beauty.

The Anthropic Principle

The general nature of the Anthropic Principle has already been presented above: we must discover how to see the roots of consciousness at the atomic level; to see what atoms and molecules must be, viewed as spirit-matter, or else we deny the very existence of consciousness. But different investigators give the Anthropic Principle various meanings, depending in general on how far they can take it comfortably. Some use it to examine the constraints on physics of the existence of biological life, some study consciousness, and a few go so far as to get into the realm of spirituality. Here, we can only show a few interesting examples.

Here is an early statement of the Anthropic Principle,

written by Teilhard around 1930, which is still one of the most far-reaching:

It is, at the root, impossible that spontaneous beings, possessing inwardness, could ever have developed from a universe presumed to have begun as matter *[conceived as deterministic]. Anyone who accepts this starting point blocks all roads that would lead [via evolution] to the present state of the universe. On the other hand, from a cosmos initially made up of* elementary freedoms *[i.e., non-deterministic atoms], we can easily deduce not only the arising of living beings, but also the* appearances of exactitude *upon which the modern mathematical physics of matter is founded.*[4]

A section of Teilhard's *Hymn of the Universe* is entitled "The Spiritual Power of Matter," which contains not only a "Hymn to Matter," but also the following exhortation:

Bathe yourself in the ocean of matter; plunge into it where it is deepest and most violent; struggle in its currents and drink of its waters. For it cradled you long ago in your pre-conscious existence; and it is that ocean that will raise you up to God.[5]

I am in full agreement with Teilhard's concern that we not stop short in facing the spiritual power of matter. The highest human values and aspirations must be seen as arising from within.

On the other hand, every level at which physicists study the Anthropic Principle makes positive contributions. Here are some examples.

In Figure App.2, as in the case of Figure App.1, the left side represents the physics that contains, or leads to, the right side, namely the facts visible in the present cosmos. The arrows may be read as "leads to." In his book *Disturbing the*

"Fine-Tuned" Universe
Physical Constants --> Life Conditions --> Life

Figure App.2

Universe, Freeman Dyson gives a relatively succinct presentation of the fine-tuned universe:

If, as seems likely, the evolution of life requires a star like the sun, supplying energy at a constant rate for billions of years, then the strength of nuclear forces had to lie within a rather narrow range to make life possible.

A similar but independent accident appears in connection with the "weak interaction," which is of just the strength so that the hydrogen in the sun burns at a slow and steady rate. If it were much different, any forms of life dependent on sunlike stars would again be in difficulties.

The facts of astronomy include some other accidents that work to our advantage. We could not have survived if the average distance between stars were only two million million miles instead of twenty.

All the rich diversity of organic chemistry depends on a delicate balance between electrical and quantum-mechanical forces. The balance exists only because the laws of physics include an "exclusion principle" which forbids two electrons to occupy the same state. There are many other lucky accidents in atomic physics. Without such accidents, water could not exist as a liquid, and chains of carbon atoms could not form complex organic molecules. There is a peculiar harmony between the structure of the universe and the needs of life and intelligence.[6]

One of the most famous of Anthropic Principle predictions was that of Fred Hoyle, who in 1953 predicted the discovery of a resonance level in helium nuclei, without which the stars would have been unable to "cook" the heavier elements that fill out the chemist's periodic table, especially carbon, the only element capable of providing the physical foundation of life. Because of this resonance level, two helium nuclei can stick together just long enough (0.0000000000000001 second) for a third helium nucleus to have a tiny chance of hitting the pair to form carbon in the core of a "red giant" star. Later that star will explode, spraying carbon into the dust of the galaxy, seeding it with the possibility of life.

Variations on the Anthropic Principle

Here, for flavor, is another pair of aspects of the Anthropic Principle. The framer of the first, John Archibald Wheeler, is known among scientists as "Mr. Universe," and is undoubtedly the greatest living cosmologist. He is also known as the educator of Nobel laureates in physics. Since it is true that physicists are beachcombers of beauty on the distant shores of knowledge, it is perhaps useful to point out that physics gives us our technology, which keeps business in business. To me, these are just more opposites merging.

The Participatory Anthropic Principle of John Archibald Wheeler states:

The observer is just as necessary for the creation of the universe, as the universe is for the existence of the observer.[7]

The Final Anthropic Principle was put forth by F. J. Tipler:

If the cosmic order implies the creation of consciousness, once consciousness arrives (not necessarily human) it can never die out.[8]

This contradicts "standard" cosmologies, and the famous Second Law of Thermodynamics, according to which "things run down." In this view, nature should not build toward consciousness except on a small scale, and early in the total life of the cosmos, and then only by accident. Fortunately, this rule is balanced by the newly recognized Anthropic Principle, which says, in effect, "Things run up." The nature of physical reality, recognized in the early cosmos, is balanced by the nature of freedom and consciousness, which we are now beginning to recognize.

Nature of Physical   **Nature of Freedom**

Reality   **<--------->**   **& Consciousness**

Wholeness = Balance of Opposites: Spirit-Matter

Figure App.3

Nothing is so important to a living being as being alive, which is by no means a reference to mere physical life. Humans have always risked physical life and physical well-being for values that weigh much more in the psyche than these, and it is these values that I am summarizing in the word *aliveness*. This is also why we have always projected some form of aliveness beyond the physical end of life. I call this the "concern with living," and I feel that this concern is the proper focus of the Anthropic Principle. It includes what various traditions refer to as spirituality. To repeat, it is this which is the proper focus of the critique of physics, to examine what Teilhard described with the expression "the spiritual power of matter."[9] We must employ all our powers of vision to see what changes in our concepts of physical reality are required.

As I structure the enterprise, the search for beauty (unified worldview) involves the enterprise of physics to discover and confirm the nonrational nature of reality. In the process, physics gives us the *mental* model for living with opposites. However, only through *living* with opposites do we experience their reality and confirm that reality existentially. When that does happen, we have a living confirmation of the unity of existence overall, which incidentally also strengthens our conviction that our physical interpretation of nature is on track.

The Anthropic Principle will eventually overturn previous attitudes, but it will take a while, just as it has taken the Anthropic Principle a while to come into acceptability as a study. It has aptly been said that physics proceeds from funeral to funeral of those who contributed major advances, but could not take new steps after that. Humans are tenacious of their preconceptions.

Notes

PREFACE, *Pages vii–xii*
1. Heisenberg 1971, 215.
2. Cytowic 1993.
3. *New York Times,* 25 May 1946.
4. Jung 1975, 109; 1968, par. 18; 1963a, par. 715. The term *corpuscles* has since been replaced in scientific parlance by the term *particles.*

INTRODUCTION, *Pages xiii–xxvi*
1. von Franz 1980.
2. Luke 17:33. See the discussion of this passage in chapter 7 below.

CHAPTER 1, *Pages 3–25*
1. Sheldrake 1995, 58; Polyani 1958.
2. Neumann 1989, 8.
3. Ibid.
4. Teilhard de Chardin 1969, 22–23.
5. von Franz 1974, 171. I have modified the syntax of this quotation slightly.
6. Cytowic 1993, 156.
7. Ibid.
8. Bloom and Lazerson 1988, 234.
9. Wheeler, in conversation at a colloquium in Madison, Wisconsin, 1992.
10. See, for example, the experiments described in Rhine 1947.
11. Jung 1969a, par. 745.
12. Jung 1969b, par. 420.
13. Neumann 1989, 9.

CHAPTER 2, *Pages 26–46*
1. Sagan 1980, 176.
2. Quoted ibid., 186.
3. Ibid., 183.

4. Ibid., 188. Emphasis mine.
5. Schwarzschild 1962, 1.
6. Galilei 1967 [1632], 145.
7. Ibid., 328.
8. von Franz 1980, ch. 3.
9. Whitehead 1969, vii,viii.
10. Schrödinger, 1953.

CHAPTER 3, *Pages 47–68*
1. French and Kennedy 1985, 224.
2. Teller 1969, 83.
3. Wilhelm and Baynes 1967, 280.
4. Ibid., 283.
5. Ibid., 289.
6. See note 12 in chapter 1 above.
7. Quoted in Kirk and Raven 1969, 114.
8. Quoted in ibid., 117.
9. Kazantzakis 1960, 43.
10. Tillich 1948, 153–163.
11. See Nagel 1958.
12. Polanyi 1958, 395–401.
13. Cropper 1970, 122.
14. French and Kennedy 1985, 325.

CHAPTER 4, *Pages 69–84*
1. See note 2 in chapter 3 above.
2. Clark 1960, 26.
3. Newton (1966 [1687]), 544–548.
4. Patchen 1969, 368.

CHAPTER 5, *Pages 85–105*
1. Moon 1970, 9.
2. Neumann 1954, 102.
3. Neumann 1989, 7.
4. Ibid., 33.
5. In Kirk and Raven 1969, 32.
6. In Munitz 1965, 26.
7. Wilhelm and Baynes 1967, 294.
8. See note 1 in this chapter.
9. von Franz 1980, 7–8.
10. Ibid., 36.

CHAPTER 6, *Pages 106–127*
1. Burke 1985, 9.
2. Deck 1978, 359.

3. Quoted in Deck 1978, 386.

4. Ashton 1992, 15.

5. Jung 1963b, par. 768.

6. Swedenborg 1934 [1764], n. 234.

7. Jung 1969a, 355–470.

8. See note 12 in chapter 1 above.

9. Jaynes 1976.

10. Jung 1963a, 98, 99.

11. Jung, 1969b, pars. 356n, 382n.

12. James 1902, 511–512. For examples of this idea in Jung, see Jung 1969a, pars. 659, 740.

13. Swedenborg 1996 [c.1752], n. 1594[5].

14. Teilhard de Chardin 1959, 53. The published title in English is *The Phenomenon of Man*, which is not only out of date as to gender language, but untrue to the French.

15. Though Jung (1969b, par. 359) traces the concept of the unconscious itself to C. G. Carus (in the first half of the nineteenth century), it is certainly present in Swedenborg, even in the little quoted above, in the reference to the "interior" and "internal" human, of which the "external" person (i.e., ego-consciousness) may not be aware, as Swedenborg says elsewhere.

16. Allen 1967, 18–19.

17. Ibid.

18. Swedenborg 1937 [1763]. Gender specific language has been altered to reflect the original Latin more accurately, capitalization has been somewhat modernized, and numbering has been added for reference.

19. This story is very engagingly told by Dole and Kirven in *A Scientist Explores Spirit* (1992, 1–6).

20. Swedenborg 1933 [1771], n. 508.

21. Hitchcock 1976.

22. Kierkegaard 1962 [1834], 46, 49.

23. Ibid., 53.

24. Cytowic 1993, ch.19.

25. Sartre 1971, 399.

26. Jung 1964, 381–382.

27. Ibid., 382.

28. Hitchcock 1976.

29. See note 12 in chapter 1 above.

30. Jung 1964, 253.

31. Neumann 1989.

CHAPTER 7, *Pages 128–145*

1. Goethe 1959 [1831], 134.

2. Jung 1971, par. 357.

3. Prigogine and Stengers 1984, 7.

4. Edinger 1973, 7.

5. See note 14 to chapter 7 above.

6. von Franz 1980, ix.

7. *Essay on Man,* Epistle 2, line 2.

8. Jung 1966, pars. 469, 470.

9. Luke 17:33. The rendering is mine.

10. Neumann 1989, 216–217.

11. Teilhard de Chardin 1969, 58.

CHAPTER 8, *Pages 146–160*

1. James 1902, 508.

2. Ibid., 515.

3. von Franz 1980, 177. The quotation is from a letter of Jung's, printed also in Jung 1973, 298.

4. Kierkegaard 1956 [1847].

5. von Franz 1980, 158, 163.

6. Teilhard de Chardin 1969, 84–85.

7. Ibid., 87.

8. Ibid., 87–88.

9. Neumann 1954, 286.

10. Ibid., 89.

11. Tillich 1952, 164.

12. In Goodchild 1981, 278.

CHAPTER 9, *Pages 161–182*

1. Weinberg 1979, 144.

2. Neumann 1989, 215.

3. Ibid., 234–235.

4. Remark made by Prigogine at Nobel Conference XXVI, Gustavus Adolphus College, St. Peter, Minnesota, 1992.

5. James 1902, 131–133, 526

6. James 1902.

7. Fowler 1981, 23.

8. Jung 1975, 66.

9. Ibid., 525.

10. Fowler 1981, 23.

11. Terence. *Heauton Timoroumenos.* I.1.25.

12. Jung 1975, 529.

13. Moon 1970, 89.

14. Seager 1993.

15. C. C. Bonney, quoted in Dole 1993, 42.

16. Dole 1993, 37–38.

17. Ibid., 43–44.

18. von Franz 1980, 16, 27.

19. These issues were presented in two earlier books. In *Atoms, Snowflakes*

and God, I described how the Patterning that guides evolution might be viewed as *unconscious omniscience*; and in *The Web of the Universe,* I gave a case for the awakening of the divine within humanity.

20. Moon 1972, 27–28.

APPENDIX, *Pages 183–194*

1. Jung 1971, par. 700.
2. Jung 1969b, par. 16.
3. Jung 1969b, par. 525
4. Teilhard de Chardin 1969, 23.
5. Teilhard de Chardin 1965, 60.
6. Dyson 1979, 250–252.
7. Balashov 1991, 1069–1076.
8. Ibid.
9. Teilhard de Chardin 1965, 55.

References

Allen, Gay Wilson. 1967. *William James: A Biography.* New York: Viking.

Ashton, Dore. 1992. *Noguchi East and West.* Berkeley: University of California Press.

Balashov, Yuri V 1991. Resource Letter AP-1: The anthropic principle. *American Journal of Physics* 59 (December): 1069–1076.

Bloom, Floyd E., and Arlyne Lazerson. 1988. *Brain, Mind, and Behavior.* New York: W. H. Freeman.

Burke, James. 1985. *The Day the Universe Changed.* Boston: Little Brown.

Clark, R.T.R. 1960. *Myth and Symbol in Ancient Egypt.* New York: Grove Press.

Cropper, William H. 1970. *The Quantum Physicists and an Introduction to Their Physics.* New York: Oxford University Press.

Cytowic, Richard E. 1993. *The Man Who Tasted Shapes.* New York: Warner Books.

Deck, Raymond. 1978. *Blake and Swedenborg.* Ann Arbor: University Microfilms International Dissertation 78-19934.

Dole, George F. 1993. *With Absolute Respect: The Swedenborgian Theology of Charles Carroll Bonney.* West Chester, Penn.: Swedenborg Foundation.

Dole, George F., and Robert H. Kirven. 1996 (1992). *A Scientist Explores Spirit.* West Chester, Penn.: Swedenborg Foundation.

Dyson, Freeman. 1979. *Disturbing the Universe*. New York: Harper and Row.

Edinger, Edward F. 1973. *Ego and Archetype*. New York: Penguin Books.

Fowler, William. 1981. *Stages of Faith*. San Francisco: HarperSanFrancisco.

French, A. P., and P. J. Kennedy., eds. 1985. *Niels Bohr: A Centennary Volume*. Cambridge: Harvard University Press.

Galilei, Galileo. 1967 [1632]. *Dialogue Concerning the Two Chief World Systems*. Berkeley: University of California Press.

Goethe, J. W. von. 1959 [1831]. *Faust*. Part Two. Translated by Philip Wayne. New York: Penguin Books.

Goodchild, Peter. 1981. *J. Robert Oppenheimer: Shatterer of Worlds*. Boston: Houghton Mifflin.

Heidegger, Martin. 1975. *Early Greek Thinking*. New York: Harper & Row.

Heisenberg, W. 1971. *Physics and Beyond*. New York: Harper and Row.

Hitchcock, John. 1976. *A Comparison of 'Complementarity' in Quantum Physics with Analogous Structures in Kierkegaard's Philosophical Writings, from a Jungian Point of View*. Ann Arbor, Mich.: University Microfilms International Dissertation 76–9150.

————. 1982. *Atoms, Snowflakes and God: The Convergence of Science and Religion*. San Francisco: Alchemy Books.

————. 1991. *The Web of the Universe: Jung, the "New Physics" and Human Spirituality*. New York: Paulist Press.

James, William. 1902. *The Varieties of Religious Experience*. New York: Penguin Classics.

Jaynes, Julian. 1976. *The Origin of Consciousness in the Breakdown of the Bicameral Mind*. Boston: Houghton-Mifflin.

Jung, C. G. 1963a. *Memories, Dreams, Reflections*. New York: Vintage.

————. 1963b. *Mysterium Coniunctionis*. The Collected Works of C.G. Jung, vol. 14. New York: Pantheon Books.

———. 1964. *Man and his Symbols*. New York: Doubleday.

———. 1966. *The Practice of Psychotherapy*. The Collected Works of C. G. Jung, vol. 16. Princeton: Princeton University Press.

———. 1968. *Psychology and Alchemy*. The Collected Works of C. G. Jung, vol. 12. Princeton: Princeton University Press.

———. 1969a. *Psychology and Religion: West and East*. The Collected Works of C. G. Jung, vol. 11. Princeton: Princeton University Press.

———. 1969b. *The Structure and Dynamics of the Psyche*. The Collected Works of C. G. Jung, vol. 8. Princeton: Princeton University Press.

———. 1971. *Psychological Types*. The Collected Works of C. G. Jung, vol. 6. Princeton: Princeton University Press.

———. 1973. *Letters 1: 1909–1950*. Princeton: Princeton University Press.

———. 1975. *Letters 2: 1951–1961*. Princeton: Princeton University Press.

Kazantzakis, Nikos. 1960. *The Saviors of God: Spiritual Exercises*. New York: Simon and Schuster.

Kierkegaard, Søren. 1956 (1847). *Purity of the Heart is to Will One Thing*. Translated by Douglas V. Steere. New York: Harper's.

———. 1962 (1834). *Philosophical Fragments*. Princeton: Princeton University Press.

Kirk, G. S., and J. E. Raven. 1969. *The Presocratic Philosophers*. Cambridge, UK: Cambridge University Press.

Moon, Sheila. 1970. *A Magic Dwells*. Middletown, Conn.: Wesleyan University Press.

———. 1972. *Joseph's Son*. Francistown, New Hampshire: Golden Quill Press.

Munitz, Milton. 1965. *Theories of the Universe*. New York: Macmillan Free Press.

Nagel, Ernest. 1958. *Gödel's Proof*. New York: New York University Press.

Neumann, Erich. 1954. *The Origin and History of Consciousness*. New York: Pantheon Books.

———. 1989. The *Place of Creation*. Princeton: Princeton University Press.

Newton, Isaac. 1966 (1687). *Principia*. Vol. 2. Translated by Andrew Motte. Revised by Florian Cajori. Berkeley: University of California Press.

Otto, Rudolf. 1958. *The Idea of the Holy*. New York: Oxford University Press.

Patchen, Kenneth. 1969. *Sleepers Awake*. New York: New Directions.

Polanyi, Michael. 1958. *Personal Knowledge*. New York: Harper Torchbooks.

Prigogine, Ilya. 1992. Lecture at Nobel Conference XXVI, St. Peter, Minn.

Prigogine, Ilya, and Isabelle Stengers. 1984. *Order out of Chaos*. New York: Bantam Books.

Rhine, J. B. 1947. *The Reach of the Mind*. New York: William Sloan Associates.

Sagan, Carl. 1980. *Cosmos*. New York: Random House.

Sartre, Jean Paul. 1971. Existentialism is humanism. Translated by Philip Mairet. In *The Existentialist Tradition: Selected Writings*. Edited by Nino Langiulli. [city], New Jersey: Humanities Press.

Schrödinger, Erwin. 1953. What Is Matter? *Scientific American* (September): 52–59.

Schwarzschild, Martin. 1962. *The Structure and Evolution of the Stars*. Princeton: Princeton University Press.

Seager, Richard II. 1993. *The Dawn of Religious Pluralism*. Chicago: Open Court.

Sheldrake, Rupert. 1995. *Seven Experiments That Could Change the World*. New York: Riverhead Books.

Swedenborg, Emanuel. 1933 (1771). *True Christian Religion*. New York: E.P. Dutton Everyman's Library. Also published by Swedenborg Foundation (2 volumes), 1996.

———. 1934 (1764). *Divine Providence.* London: The Swedenborg Society. Also published by Swedenborg Foundation, 1995.

———. 1937 (1763). *Divine Love and Wisdom.* London: The Swedenborg Society. Also published by Swedenborg Foundation, 1995.

———. 1996–1998 (c. 1752). *Arcana Coelestia.* 12 volumes. Translated by John Clowes. Revised by John F. Potts. West Chester, Penn.: Swedenborg Foundation.

Teilhard de Chardin, Pierre. 1959. *The Phenomenon of Man.* New York: Harper Torchbooks.

———. 1965. *Hymn of the Universe.* New York: Harper and Row.

———. 1969. *Human Energy.* New York: Harcourt Brace Jovanovich.

Teller, Edward. 1969. Neils Bohr and the Idea of Complementarity. In *Great Men of Physics.* Edited by Marvin Chachere. Los Angeles: Tinnon-Brown.

Tillich, Paul. 1948. *The Shaking of the Foundations.* New York: Charles Scribner's Sons.

———. 1952. *The Courage to Be.* New Haven: Yale University Press.

von Franz, Marie-Louise. 1974. *Number and Time.* Evanston: Northwestern University Press.

———. 1980. *Projection and Recollection in Jungian Psychology.* La Salle, Ill.: Open Court.

Weinberg, Steven. 1979. *The First Three Minutes.* New York: Bantam Books.

Werfel, Franz. 1976. *Star of the Unborn.* New York: Bantam Books.

Whitehead, Alfred North. 1969. *Process and Reality.* New York: Macmillan Free Press.

Wilhelm, Richard, and Cary F. Baynes, trans. 1967. *The I Ching, or Book of Changes.* Princeton: Princeton University Press (Bollingen Series XIX).

Index

Abelard, Pierre, 77
acausal orderedness. See *causality*.
Albertus Magnus, 77
aliveness, xxi, xxv, 124, 142–145, 166, 193. See also *living*.
Anaximander, 8, 53–55
apeiron. See *Anaximander*.
Answer to Job [Jung], 23,114
anthropic principle, 44, 183–194
archaic identity, xxiii, 98, 130–131, 178
Aristotle, 32, 53, 66, 121
art, artists, vii, 92, 110–111, 117, 125
awakening
  ego, 101–104, 130–131, 140, 143
  God's xxv, 180
  Ionian, 29–31

Bacon, Roger, 77
barbarism, 129
Blake, William, 3, 110–111
Bohr, Niels, xvi, xxi, 35–36, 48, 61–63, 122–127
Bonney, Charles Carroll, 175–176, 178
Book of Changes. See *I Ching*.
bootstrap process, 130
Brahe, Tycho, xvi, 34–35
Bruno, Giordano, 120–121
Burke, James, 106

causality, x, 16, 81, 82;
  and acausal orderedness, 18
centroversion, xxiv, 155, 157
cerebral cortex, 12, 17–18, 22, 124

Clark, R.T.R, 74
Coleridge, Samuel Taylor, 110–111, 115
complementarity, xvi–xviii, xxi, 37–40, 47–52, 58, 63–65, 108–109, 111, 165–166
  ancient, 50–54
  defined, 49
  and Kierkegaard, 122–124
  and Swedenborg, 118–120
  of psychology and physics, 125–127
complexity, complexification, 138, 151, 179
conflict. See *opposites.*
consciousness, xv, xx–xxi, xxiii, xxiv–xxv, 6, 13, 24, 40, 44, 85–87, 89, 91, 92–95, 97, 100, 103–104, 113–114, 127, 129, 130, 131, 140, 141, 154, 157, 162, 179, 180, 184–185, 193
  evolution of, 85–105
  gathering, 97, 138–141
  God's, xxv, 6
  See also *ego.*
Copernicus, Nicholas, 33–34, 120
cosmos (physical aspect of universe). See *universe.*
crucifixion, 142
cultures, evolution of. See *evolution.*
Cytowic, Richard, ix, 17, 21

Darwin, Charles, 121
death, 75, 89, 96, 114, 116, 142, 153–155, 157, 158, 172, 174, 180
death/rebirth, xxiii, 143–145
depth;
  human, xiv, xxiv, 13, 87, 97, 130, 136, 151, 158
  potentially infinite, 101, 107
  of reality, xxiv, 83, 97, 104, 117
Descartes, Rene, 76, 80–81, 121
Dickinson, Emily, 106
distancing, xv, 18, 96, 115
divine;
  eclipse of, xix, 73–78
  love and wisdom, viii, xxi, 112, 118–120
  within the human, 87, 102–105, 115–117, 143, 158–159, 162
duality;
  wave/particle, xi, 8, 39, 44, 125
  See also *electrons, electrons and photons, opposites.*
Dyson, Freeman, 191

Edinger, Edward F., 130
ego;
egocentricity, 101, 104, 113
  ego-consciousness, xiv–xv, 6, 8–12, 17, 25, 60, 63, 65, 86–87, 89, 90,
    91, 113–116, 129, 144, 168, 185
  mere-ego, 163–164
Egypt, ancient, 74–75, 166–167
Einstein, Albert, x, xvi, 36–37, 39, 62, 72, 82, 100, 165
electrons, xi, xviii, 8–9, 24, 36–37, 39, 52, 60–65, 67
  and photons, 7, 44–45, 48–49, 78
Eliot, T.S., 150
Enlightenment,The, xiv, 78–80, 87
evolution;
  of consciousness. See *consciousness*.
  cultural, xxi, 106–110. See also *facts, role of.*
  of life, xxv, 17, 21, 78, 79, 90, 96, 112–114, 121, 141, 178–180,
    183–199

facts, role of, ix, x, xxii, 12, 36–37, 43–44, 48, 57–58, 65–66, 82, 121,
    169–170, 180
field, xiv, 3, 4–7, 7–10, 10–13, 16, 18–19, 21–25, 65, 86, 101, 114, 138,
    144, 179;
  field-knowledge, 17, 91–92
  morphogenetic, 7
  physical, 3, 7
  See also *patterning, worldfield.*
forgiveness, xxiv, 152–155, 157–158, 181
  forgiving the universe, 151–160
Fowler, James, 170–171, 173
freedom, 4, 14, 27–28, 114, 124, 129, 141, 144, 156, 162;
  and conflict of opposites. See *opposites.*
  and ego-consciousness, xv–xvi, xix, 12, 70, 83, 94, 98, 133, 141
  and God, 113–114, 162
  sacrifice of, 12–13

Galilei, Galileo, xvi, 32–34, 37, 120–121
gastrulation, gastrointestinal tract, xxiii, 134–138;
  and ego (spiritual), 136
God;
  excluded from "scientific knowledge", 77–81
  images of, viii, x, xiv, xv, 102, 112–114, 118, 119–120, 129, 154, 158,
    167, 168, 171, 172
  as ground of being, 69, 146

realm (kingdom) of, xxiv, 148–151
  as self-reflexive. See *self-reflexivity, God's*.
  as unconscious, xxv, 6, 114
  as unity of opposites, xxv, 113, 124, 161
  as the Unknown, 123, 149, 172
  as waiting, xxiv, 158, 178–182
Gödel, Kurt, 58
good/evil. See *opposites, specific*.
gravity, 7, 81, 82
ground of being. See *God*.

Heisenberg, Werner, 62, 63, 126
Hesiod, 95, 162
Hoyle, Fred, 191
humanity, deeper, viii, xii, xviii, xxiv–xxv, 24, 42, 78, 84, 137–139, 152,
    156, 162, 165, 173, 181
hydrogen atom, 60–61

I Ching, or *Book of Changes*, xvii, 8, 50–52, 96
individuality, individuation, xxii, xxiv, 20, 23, 105, 131, 148, 151–152
infantile omnipotence, xxiii, 98
inner, inwardness, xiv, xxii–xxiii, 19, 22, 116, 120, 131–133, 138–139,
    155–156, 190;
  inner/outer. See *opposites, specific*.
  the "within of things," 116, 139
involution, xxiii, 133–137. See also *patterning, worldfield*.

James, Henry, Sr., 117–118
James, William, 115, 118, 146, 147, 169
Jaynes, Julian, 114
Jefferson, Thomas, 79
Jesus of Nazareth, xxiii, 102, 143, 148, 149, 150, 176, 181–182
Jordan, Pascual, 125
Jung, C.G., ix, xi–xii, xv, xxi, 14, 18, 23, 52, 102, 109–115, 120, 123,
    124–127, 129–131, 142, 172, 173–174, 184–186;
  and science, 124–127, 185–186

Kant, Immanuel, 42
Kazantzakis, Nikos, 55
Kepler, Johannes, xvi, 32, 34–35, 72, 100, 121
Kierkegaard, Søren, xii, xxi, 109, 117, 122–124, 125, 127, 149, 150

La Place, Pierre, 81

limbic system (of the brain), 17
living, viii, ix, xiv, xxiii, xxv, xxvi, 10, 20, 43, 59, 67, 75, 104–105,
    123–124, 128–130, 136–137, 140, 141–142, 143–145, 154, 156–157,
    159, 170, 174, 193. See also *aliveness, divine, universe.*
love, ix, xv, xxiv, 43, 95, 102–105, 129, 152, 162, 167, 181–182
Lucretius, 79

Maori, xx, 90–91, 93
mathematics, 16, 19, 30, 38–39, 58–59, 75, 188, 190
meaning, xv, xx, 6, 15–19, 23, 41, 48, 59, 71, 88–90, 101–104, 131, 137,
    154, 163, 166, 171–172
"mechanics and mystics", xvi, 28–37
monotheism, 161, 167–174;
radical, 170–174
Moon, Sheila, 88, 97, 180–182
moral dimension, 10, 87, 129, 155, 178
"mystics." See *"mechanics and mystics."*
myth, mythic motifs, xx, 38, 54, 78, 85–105, 174
  Egyptian, 78, 93–94
  Maori, 90–91, 93

naturalism, 31, 129
Neumann, Erich, xv, 11, 25, 90–91, 114, 127, 144, 155, 163–164
Newton, Isaac, 39, 81–82, 100
Niebuhr, H. Richard, 170
Noguchi, Isamu, 111
nonrational. See *rational/nonrational.*
numen, numinous, numinosity, xix, xxiv, 66, 80, 87–90, 92, 100, 141, 164

obstacles, 156–157
open, opening, openness, xiv, xx, xxii–xxiii, xxiv, 12, 40, 89–95, 101, 105,
    124, 130, 133, 134–137, 159, 161, 162. See also *involution.*
Oppenheimer, J. Robert, 159
opposites;
  central, for living, 6, 47, 55
  holding, 129
  as source of freedom, 112, 124, 129
  unity of, 47. See also *field.*
  conflict of, 77–80, 129, 184
opposites, specific;
  heart/mind, 6, 55, 150
  inner/outer, xv, xxii–xxiii, 6, 10, 18, 19–20, 23, 59, 85, 101, 127,
      128–132, 137

masculine/feminine, 93, 119, 124
matter/spirit, 6, 9, 55. See also *spirit–matter.*
good/evil, 10, 112–114, 158–159, 174
rational/nonrational, xviii, 56, 58
self/other, 6, 133
universal/unique, xxii
Origen, 128, 130–131
Otto, Rudolf, 88

pain, suffering, 87, 100, 124, 151–154, 156, 181–182
paradox, x–xii, xviii, 20, 55, 89, 108, 122–124, 128–129, 162, 166
particles. See *electron, photon, duality.*
Patchen, Kenneth, 47, 83
patterning, viii, 5–6, 101, 162
Pauli, Wolfgang, ix, xxi, 125
photons. See *electrons and photons.*
physics, viii, ix, xv, xviii, 8, 9, 23, 30–31, 37, 48, 58, 62, 65, 81, 122, 164,
    166, 183–184 (see also *science, standard science*);
parallels with psychology, 124–127, 185–186
pluralism, religious, xxvi, 174–178
Polanyi, Michael, 7, 59
polarities. See *opposites.*
Pope, Alexander, 141
Prigogine, Ilya, 129, 166
projection, xx, 22, 38, 97–102, 104, 132–133, 136, 139–141. See also
    archaic identity.
psyche, psychic, xix, xxiii, 13, 15, 18, 24, 38, 40, 43, 53, 56, 57, 69,
    95–96, 104, 109, 112–113, 115, 120, 123, 125, 126, 127, 141, 143,
    145, 151, 183–186, 193. See also *spirit/psyche/matter triad.*
Pythagoras, Pythagoreans, xvi, 29, 34–35

quantifiability, 65, 137. See also *measurement.*
quantum state, 64

rational/nonrational. See *opposites, specific.*
rationalism, reductionism, viii, x, xv, xvi–xvii, xviii–xix, xxi, xxiv, xxv, 14,
    31, 37–40, 42–44, 45, 56–60, 66–68, 70–73, 76, 79, 80–84, 115,
    163–164, 178, 188
reality, xxiv, xxv, 10;
    alignment with, 43, 161, 179
    physical, x, xxii;
        images of, 12–13, 17, 25, 30, 35, 38–39, 107, 110, 123, 170
        measurable, measurement, xix, 23, 62–65, 72–73, 74, 105, 108, 137

nonrational, paradoxical, viii, x, xv, xxv, 43, 58, 108, 124, 149, 162, 166, 179, 189, 193
physical and spiritual aspects equally real, 193–194
psychic, 25, 57, 126
wholeness of, ix, 44, 60, 101
rebirth. See *death/rebirth.*
reductionism. See *rationalism.*
relativity, Einsteinian, 23, 36, 39, 72
religion, xv, xviii–xix, xxiv–xxvi, 5, 30, 31, 34, 37, 70, 74, 75, 76, 79–80, 85, 89, 92, 109, 117, 121, 137–138, 142, 167, 168–178, 186;
as binding back together, 138, 146–160
See also *science and religion, religious pluralism.*
resonance, 100–101, 192

Sagan, Carl, xvi, 28–30
Sartre, Jean–Paul, 124
Schwarzschild, Martin, 26, 30–31, 43
science;
standard, xv, 15, 32, 37, 41, 42–43, 59–60, 65, 83, 137, 163, 183
and spirituality (or religion), xiii–xiv, xviii–xix, xxi, 25, 26–28, 74, 92, 97, 109, 124–125, 127;
convergence of, vii, xviii–xix, xxi, xxv, 69, 82, 84, 106, 112, 117, 125, 130, 133, 161, 164
divergence of, xviii–xix, 69–84, 111
seeing, viii–ix, xv, xix, 10, 20, 65, 69–72, 80, 87, 89, 100, 102, 106–107, 132, 141–142, 155, 165, 181
Self (archetype, regulating center of psyche), xxiii, 86, 100–104, 131, 133, 148, 151, 163–164
self-reflexivity, 6, 85, 130, 141, 150, 158, 171;
God's, 171–172, 180
shadow, 129, 159, 174
Sheldrake, Rupert, 7
special creation xxv, 13–14, 97, 178, 183
spirit, spiritual, spirituality, xv, xx, xxiii, xxiv, 3, 42, 65, 70, 77, 81–84, 94, 97, 99, 105, 109, 111, 112, 116, 118, 123, 127, 134, 137, 143, 146–147, 150, 161, 163, 165, 168, 171, 181, 186–187, 189–190, 193;
spirit and matter, xx, 14, 24, 48, 52, 81, 86, 94–95, 105, 109, 113, 171, 184, 185, 189
spirit–matter, xiv, xxi, 6, 9, 24, 55, 65, 111, 113–114, 139, 171–172, 179, 187, 189, 193
spirit/psyche/matter triad, 53, 95–96, 105, 185–186, 189
spirits, spiritual powers, 99, 111

spiritualism, 32, 115–116, 118
  See also *science and spirituality*.
suffering. See *pain*
Suzuki, D.T., 175
Swedenborg, Emanuel, vii, viii, ix, xxi, 109–122, 123–124, 127, 129, 141,
  175
symbols, symbolism, 8–9, 17, 34, 35, 40, 50–51, 67, 86, 91, 93, 100,
  102–105, 112–113, 115, 139, 153, 165, 167
synchronicity, xv, 15–19, 59, 86, 101, 171;
  and emotion, 16
synesthesia, 21

t'ai chi t'u (yin-yang symbol), 9, 50, 133
Teilhard de Chardin, Pierre, xxi, 14, 24, 65, 116, 139, 145, 152–153,
  155–156, 187, 190, 193
Teller, Edward, 49, 71
Terence, 173
Thales, xvi, 29, 31, 53, 71
thought experiments, 32
Tillich, Paul, xvii, 56, 157
Tipler, F.J., 192
transformation, personal, 38, 75, 87, 142, 151, 153
Tulk, C.A., 110

unconscious, unconsciousness, xxii, 10, 18, 23, 31, 47, 57, 79, 85–86, 91,
  97, 116, 126, 131, 139–140, 143, 154, 157, 178, 184
unitary reality. See *unus mundus*
universals, universality, xxii, 16, 20, 111, 117–118, 122–123, 126, 158,
  172, 173, 175
universe, cosmos, xxv–xxvi, 3, 5–6, 14, 25, 30, 40, 41, 44, 65–66, 97, 102,
  103, 122–123, 124, 138, 161, 162, 163, 179–180, 183–184;
  universe sets problems that only love can solve, xxiv, xxvi, 142, 160, 162,
  165
  taking the universe inside, 128–145
unus mundus, unitary reality, xiii–xv, 4, 13–15, 109, 111, 127, 146

von Franz, Marie-Louise, xiii, 14, 99, 125–126, 140, 147–148, 151, 178

Watterson, Bill, 99
wave/particle duality. See *duality*.
Weinberg, Steven, 163
Wheeler, John Archibald, 23, 192
Whitehead, A.N., 42

wholes, wholeness, viii, xviii, xix, xxi, xxiv, 4, 8–9, 11, 23–24, 38, 45–46, 47–48, 55, 58–60, 65, 70–71, 77, 83–84, 90, 95, 101, 103, 120, 127, 131, 141–142, 146, 150, 153, 155, 168–170, 174, 183

worldfield, viii, xiv–xvi, xx, xxiii, 3–25, 49, 50, 54, 85, 104, 106, 113, 127, 147. See also *field.*

worldview;
  changes in, ix, xvii, 37–38, 40–44, 57
  and myth, 38, 54
  specific worldviews
    complementarity, 47–68, 109, 114, 162
    crystal spheres, 26–27, 170
    Newtonian, 39, 81–82
    rationalistic, viii, x, xvi, xviii, 14, 37, 40–44, 57–58, 76, 178, 188

yin-yang (philosophy and symbolism), xvii, 8–9, 50–52, 96. See also *I Ching* and *t'ai chi t'u.*